GO RIDE FAR

Go Ride Far

*Practical know-how from
the running, riding, writing veterinarian by*

Melinda Newton, DVM

Singletrack Press

ISBN: 9781687090256

Cover design, interior design, and composition by: Melinda Newton

Go Ride Far: Practical know-how from the running, riding, writing veterinarian is published by Singletrack Press, Yuba City CA, 95991

Text set in Palatino Linotype

SINGLETRACK PRESS

For Kathy Sherman. Thanks for making me feel welcome from the very beginning.

CONTENTS

Before You Begin

THE MAJORITY OF the content in this book are blog posts written over the last 10 years. Some are from before I was a veterinarian, some were written while I was in veterinary school, and some are from afterwards when I could claim the title Doctor. I've edited where appropriate for clarity and accuracy and added notes to others.

Nothing in this book should be considered medical advice. Although I've done my best to provide accurate information, please use common sense and implement any tips or recommendations given here at your own risk.

Introduction

WITH OVER 1,600 posts written over more than a decade, the Dr. Mel Newton blog is full of stories, tips and tricks, how-to's, educational articles, and lessons learned as a horse owner, endurance rider, and veterinarian. This collection puts all the best posts, including never-before published material, into a volume that can be read anywhere and anytime.

When selecting the posts to include in this book, I chose the ones I would want my past self to read *before* she did her first endurance ride. I'd want my past self to know from the very beginning how to back a trailer, why following someone else's conditioning plan won't work, and when it's OK to give up on an equine partner that's not a good fit for endurance. I would also want her to buy those ride pictures from her first endurance ride because she's going to love them, even though she isn't going to finish that ride, or any of the others that she tries to do that year. Yes, I really was that dumb! I didn't buy any pictures from my first season because I had decided pictures would be a reward for completed rides only.

I would also want my past self to know that it gets better — a *lot* better — and she's going to achieve all those lofty goals she set for herself, but since those are all spoilers I'll settle on telling her to keep everything simple, carry an extra stirrup in her crew bag, and practice her trot-outs at home. Above all, I want to give my discouraged, lonely past self a giant hug after that awful first ride[1] and tell her that this sport is actually pretty awesome. While it's never easy, it's definitely worthwhile.

---

1. *Yes, I tell that story in this book. For the first time ever. I wasn't able to gather the emotional energy to write it up on the blog, which was started several years after this first ride.*

My First Ride

THERE ARE BLESSED few pictures of me at my first endurance ride. I stood out even in a sport known for its wacky and off-the-wall, anything-goes culture. It wasn't just my horse, a giant black Standardbred in a sea of reasonably-sized Arabians; it was *everything*. From my American Civil-War era reproduction tack, to the tall cavalry boots I wore, to the crumbling homemade energy bars I had stuffed into a grain bag attached to my reproduction accurate-in-every-detail 1859 saddle, I didn't fit in.

Up to that point in my life, I had failed at very few things. School had been easy for me. I had gotten into the college of my choice. Then, after graduation I had my pick of several job offers. When I decided to run a marathon in my late teens, I dug deep and finished on my first try — even if it wasn't a pretty finish. I had never actually spectacularly *failed* at something I wanted badly.

I remember being so proud of my beautiful mare and her big trot when I arrived at my very first endurance ride. I imagined people turning to each other and saying, "Did you see that big black mare? Doesn't she look *good*?" To facilitate this, I hand-trotted her up and down the gravel road behind ridecamp so that everyone could see how different and special she was. I don't remember any other specifics, but I'm sure I blathered on to anyone who would listen about how she was an off-the-track Standardbred, given to me last year, and I just *knew* she was a 100-mile horse, and yes, this was our first 50-mile race.

I had picked out this ride as my endurance debut by virtue of the weekend it fell on, not because of any consideration for the characteristics of this particular course. This 50-mile event was merely the warm up; I had my sights set on a 100-mile ride that summer. For the last year I had been conditioning and planning my ride schedule which took me from first 50-mile completion to 100-mile finisher in a mere four months.

This combination of vanity and naivety is incredibly embarrassing. Can't we just pretend that I played it cool at that first ride? Pretend I didn't make a fool out of myself? I wasn't going to finish one of the toughest, most technical 50-mile rides in my region, and everyone knew it except me. But there I was, prancing around ridecamp like a silly idiot. Just like everyone else that weekend, a decade later my present self would like to turn away from that girl and pretend I had nothing to do with that clueless newbie.

I started the ride at the back to avoid the chaos of the start. This was perhaps the only good decision I made the entire ride. For the first 35 technical miles we walked where we had to and trotted where we could. We were both having fun, but by the afternoon vet check we were both tired. I had a strong gut feeling that we should call it a day.

I did not listen to this gut feeling, so I did not make the best decision of the weekend and ask for a rider option to end my ride at 35 miles. Instead, I headed out on the last 15-mile loop because a friend told me to, and that was louder than my gut.

The next ten miles were hell. We moved slowly because my horse was, in fact, completely and totally *done*. Eventually another horse and rider caught up to us and we moved a little faster for a couple of miles. But when the other rider decided it was time to move faster and leave us, his stallion refused to leave my mare. The rider, incredibly frustrated, swore at me and was eventually able to get his stud down the trail away from us, and we were by ourselves again. Then came the hill. Straight up for at least a mile, wide and exposed in the sun. Minx and I would manage a few steps, and then we'd stop to let her pant, and me puke in a patch of shade.

About half-way up the hill I noticed a small amount of blood running out of her nostrils, and I knew I had really screwed up. I was out there by myself in the middle of nowhere, puking on the side of the trail, and now my horse was going to fall over dead from my stupidity.   I sat down on the side of the trail and cried. Endurance was so much harder and a lot more lonely than I had thought it would be. I had prepared for this ride by poring over a handful of endurance riding websites (this was before Facebook), reading as many stories online as I could find, and pestering my aunt, who had done a handful of 50-mile rides, to give me advice. None of the ride stories I had read even came close to describing this level of failure. Was I the only one struggling? Was I the only one with an epic failure? Was I the only one *who was* an epic failure?

We made it to the top of the hill, and it was a little cooler up there. Slowly, we walked to the next vet check. Minx started to look better, and I decided to mount back up since I was feeling more and more ill. I had been mounted for a whole ten minutes, my first riding break in three hours, when the drag rider finally caught us. He ordered me off my horse, explaining that I needed to do my share. I was too tired to talk — an amazing level of tiredness for those of you who know me in real life — so I dismounted without arguing.

My tall, brown riding boots were totally unsuitable for endurance riding or walking trails, something they proved some miles later when I forded a water-filled ditch that was thigh-high, and the glue holding the soles on my boots came off. My boots literally fell apart on my feet. I walked down the trail in my muddy socks into the vet check, and I was pulled for being overtime. Even the veterinarian had left.

I didn't know it then, but my mare had also bowed[2] both front superficial digital flexor tendons in the effort. My next two attempts to complete 50-mile rides a month later would be lameness pulls, and that completed my first season in endurance. Not a single completion and a broken horse.

I've made a lot of mistakes over the years since that first ride, and I unabashedly blogged about most of them. What made that first ride such a bitter pill to swallow? Part of it was how utterly alone I felt. I can't be the only first-time endurance rider who was absolutely crushed by the reality of their first endurance ride, but it sure felt like it at the time. That is one of the reasons why, when I started the blog, I promised myself and my readers that I would always share honestly about both my successes and my failures. Not everyone fails as spectacularly as I did in the beginning, but if you do, learn from your mistakes and pass grace to the ones that come behind

---

2. *A form of tendonitis and a common injury in sport horses.*

you.

Many years later I implemented the practice of choosing the three best and three worst things as a post-event analysis. I call it "Nailed it, Failed it." Besides blogging and journaling, it's the best way to clearly see where I need to improve and to celebrate how far I've come. Sticking to just three in each category forces me to narrow my focus to the most important things, and it's easy to review past events and see patterns.

Nailed it

I'll be honest. Finding three things to celebrate during this ride is hard.

1. Started the ride at the back to avoid chaos. Minx started the ride calmly, despite being an ex-racehorse.

2. No tack issues. There were no rubs, galls, or soreness. Honestly, I can't remember if all four shoes stayed on, but it was very unusual for that mare to lose shoes, so I think it wasn't a problem. Despite the unconventional tack I had, it worked for us.

3. I stayed on. This mare was rather athletic and had a combination of spook, spin, and bolt that was an absolute killer for me staying on. She dumped me about once a month, but I managed to stay on her for the ride.

Failed it

Oh, where to start. Just three things?

1.   Not following my gut and pulling her at the lunch check
      when I knew in my heart she was done.

2.   Not finding a way to reach out and stay connected with
      other endurance people after my pull. I'm an introvert,
      Facebook wasn't a big thing in endurance, and I hadn't
      discovered the magic of blogging. Endurance is the *best*, but
      it can also be a little difficult to break into in my
      geographical area. I spent that ride, and my first couple of
      seasons, feeling really alone and isolated.

3.   I chose the wrong ride. This horse needed to do an LD first.
      I managed to choose one of the hardest 50s in my region
      and tried to make it work because it fit my schedule the
      best. Oops.

Did I repeat some of these mistakes? I sure did. Did I learn from
them too? YES! Well, eventually. Maybe you are a faster learner
than I was. Practicing honest post-event analysis will help.

Dear Greenbean

NOTE FROM DR. Mel: This post was written 12 years after the debacle of that first endurance ride of the last chapter.

Hey You, trying to get your horse up to a trail ride of double digit mileage for the first time. Yes, you in the corner who did a long ride last weekend in the stunning time of...3 mph. Do you feel an eternity away from the miles and pace of an endurance ride?

I'm here to reassure you that you are on the right track. I'm writing this to remind myself that I'm on the right track too.

You see, it's been a long, long, long time since I brought along a newbie horse in this sport.

I forgot just how "baby" those baby steps are in the beginning.

I did a ten-mile loop on MerryLegs[3] last week. It was a moderate-difficulty, single-track loop. It took forever.

---

3. *My then young Arabian mare.*

I understand why people make entering a Limited Distance[4] (LD) ride a two or three year plan because OMG, at this point that's how long I feel like it's going to take me to get this horse past 10 miles at 3 mph.

As a runner I've taken myself to the marathon distance and beyond, I've helped other people do the same, and I've taken at least five horses from zero to endurance-paced rides[5] of 25 or more miles (although not all made it to official endurance rides). But it's been a while. I forgot just how slow it is the beginning. Itty bitty teensy tiny imperceptible steps towards someday doing an endurance ride.

The amazing thing is that sooner than could possibly be predicted at this moment of "10 miles at 3 mph is maximum effort something happens. Suddenly you are floating down the trail averaging 7 mph, and the miles and hours are flying by. You realize that the LD goal isn't two years away. It's a "this year goal" and a fifty mile ride isn't that far behind.

Preparing for a goal is not a straight line of work and effort that gradually leads you to 50 or 100 miles. It's a roller coaster, a

---

4. *Limited distance rides are endurance competition rides offered by AERC that are less than 50 miles in length, typically 25-25 miles.*

5. *Endurance rides through the AERC are based on finishing 100 miles in 24 hours. So you have 12 hours to finish 50 miles, six hours to finish 25 miles etc. The ride time includes mandatory holds where the horse rests and is evaluated by a veterinarian, so the actual time available to ride the mileage is less than stated. Typically you must ride at least 6 mph in order to complete the ride within the specified amount of time.*

logarithmic curve. It's magic.[6]

I'm trying to savor these early rides. Once a horse has done endurance it doesn't matter if it has time off. It's never quite like starting from scratch. Right now the thought that we will be doing endurance is hilarious. One hundred miles in 24 hours? HYSTERICAL notion. We are spooking at pee rivers. Giving culverts a hard eye. Bonking[7] at least once per hour. Declaring ourselves starving at mile three.

I'm building myself an endurance partner one ride, lead-line run, arena session, carrot, and trailer ride at a time. At the same time I'm putting faith in the culmination of small steps that are leading to somewhere worth going.

Right now we are getting there at....3 mph.

---

6. *Yes, literally magic. I still can't quite fathom how I'm able to run or ride 100 miles. Or how the training that we do adds up to 50 or 100 miles? Even now – having done it multiple times – it's still magic every single time it all comes together.*

7. *The self pitying moment where you are sure you cannot go on physically, but it's actually your brain lying to you. Very manageable and fixable. Yes, I'll cover this later in the book.*

How to Back a Trailer

BACKING A TRAILER is an essential skill. Whether you have to put your trailer into a back-in-only angled parking spot at the barn, make a U-turn at a T-intersection because you took a wrong turn, navigate a tight ridecamp, or turn around in your best friend's driveway, knowing how to back a trailer is something you can't afford to put off any longer.

There is one simple trick, and two skills you need to master now.

I'm not going to lie. Certain truck and trailer combinations are easier to maneuver and back-up than others. My standard-cab, long-bed pickup combined with a bumper-pull horse trailer was an absolute dream. I could wriggle my three-horse trailer anywhere. The Dodge mega-cab, 4-door, turns-like-a-cruise-liner truck paired with any-sized trailer is an exercise in patience and near misses. I constantly misjudge the semi-truck room it needs to maneuver, but the concepts are exactly the same for both. You are going to have to practice to get a feel of your particular rig, but my "trick" and the execution of the two basic skills are exactly the same whether you have a goose-neck, bumper pull, long-bed truck, or short-bed truck.

The Trick

Don't try to figure out the physics of why the truck is doing X while the trailer is doing Y. Just do this.

Put your hand at the bottom of the steering wheel.

As you are backing up, move your hand in the direction you want the back of the trailer to go.

If you need the back of the trailer to move towards your driver's side door, move your hand in that direction.

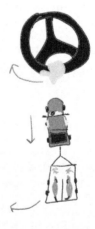

If you need the trailer to move towards the passenger side door, move your hand in that direction.

Congrats. You now have all the knowledge you need to do the two basic skills that make you look like a bad-ass in 99% of the situations.

By the way, this works whether you are looking over your shoulder or using your mirrors. Keep your hand at the bottom of the wheel and move it towards the direction you want the trailer to go. That's it!

Skill 1: Backing Up in a Straight Line

The goal is to do this:

Invariably, this ends up happening:

To correct the trailer and continue moving in a straight line just move your hand in the opposite direction of the trailer to bring the trailer back into line. In the drawing above the trailer is being naughty and is going towards the driver's side. I want it to go straight, so I move my hand towards the passenger side to make the back of the trailer move that direction.

Continue to make little corrections to counteract the trailer's goal of running itself off the road. Voila! You can now drive the trailer forwards AND backwards.

Skill 2: Backing the Trailer Around a Corner

If you can back around a 90-degree turn, you can do anything. You can turn around on a residential street at any intersection while staying in your own lane and minimally disrupting traffic. You can back into a parking spot at the barn, even if you only have a foot of clearance on either side between other trailers. You can position yourself at the trailhead so that you are less likely to be blocked in, and you can leave quickly if needed.

Backing the trailer around a turn is exactly like backing up in a straight line, except you are going to let the trailer turn gradually before correcting it back into a straight line.

Here's our plan for what we want to happen.

Now let's do it.

First you are going to back in a straight line making small adjustments until you come to the corner.

The exact moment you need to start your corner depends on your truck-trailer combination. That's why you need to practice. However, if you waited too late to start making the turn just stop, pull forward, and try again.

In this scenario you need to make a turn towards the passenger side, so move your hand towards the passenger side and allow the trailer to move in that direction.

If the trailer is turning too fast or too sharply, move your hand the other way to move the back of the trailer towards the other direction.

In the picture above, the trailer is moving too sharply towards the passenger side. I correct this by moving my hand towards the driver's side. This will slightly straighten the trailer and keep it from jack-knifing.

At some point the trailer is going to complete the turn and be oriented in the right direction. Yay!!!!!!! You don't need the trailer to keep moving towards the passenger side. Now it's time to move the trailer back towards the driver side until everything is straight behind the truck again.

Remember how to move the trailer towards the driver side? Move your hand towards the driver side.

This is why you can't think about it too hard. You are actually straightening out the truck and trailer. By doing this, the truck is actually moving around the turn to come into line with the trailer, but you don't have to worry about that. All you have to remember is that you don't need the trailer to move any further towards the passenger door; now you need the trailer to move towards your driver door so that everything is straight again. So just move your hand towards the driver door while backing up. Like magic, everything will come into line.

As you bring the trailer back into line towards the driver door, you will eventually end up straight, with the trailer in line with the truck. Now you don't need to bring the back of the trailer towards the driver door any more, so bring your hand back to center. If the trailer tries to come too far towards the driver side and you have to counteract it (what usually happens), move it back to the passenger side.

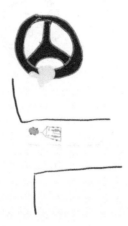

Now it's time to go find a big open area and practice.

What if none of this makes sense?

Even if it's hard for you to visualize on paper, I want you to go out and just try it. Don't think about it. Put your hand on the bottom of the wheel and start backing up. Move your hand towards the passenger door so it's in the 3 o'clock position. Watch how the trailer moved the same direction. Move your hand towards the driver door in the 9 o'clock position. Watch how the trailer starts to move in the other direction. The trailer straightens behind your truck and then continues to move towards the driver's side door. Don't crank the wheel wildly back and forth, and don't move your hand from the bottom as you swing it from one direction to the other.

You *can* do it!!!!!!!!!

Trailer Mishaps

WEIRD STUFF CAN happen even if you inspect your trailer regularly, keep up on the tires, peek at the floors, and make sure your lights work. Keep doing all these things. That way when you have mishaps they are much more interesting.

Both of the times my trailer almost gave me a heart attack it had to do with the rear doors.

My first horse trailer was an older two-horse straight load with a big, heavy, steel ramp that lifted to form part of the solid back of the trailer, courtesy of giant springs. One evening, getting ready to haul home, one of those giant springs gave up the ghost and tore free of the ramp on one side along with the hinge on that side.

The ramp twisted up above the floor of the horse trailer on the broken side while still firmly anchored on the opposite side. Not only did a horse have to navigate an awkward sidewise angled ramp to get in the trailer, all fingers had to be crossed that a fragile leg didn't slip into the hazardous gap created between the floor and ramp. The steel and spring construction of the ramp was so stiff that the ramp angle wouldn't budge, no matter how I pounded or jumped on it.

With no cell reception and a three hour drive home, I asked my saint of a Standardbred mare to load up. She did, and I somehow managed to wrench the very heavy, crooked ramp back into position and fasten it securely for the drive home. My mare unloaded herself at home with a maturity she never bothered to demonstrate on the trail, and I decided no more ramps that were integral to the door.

Of course, a ramp may have prevented my doors from swinging open 10 years later, on a different ramp-less horse trailer, all because of the lack of a single bolt.

On a rainy January morning, I trailered a young horse to a friend's house up a winding rough road.

"My worst nightmare," sums up the incident perfectly, except that by sheer luck everything turned out just fine, and we all can learn a lesson without a huge tragedy.

I pulled into the driveway to drop my mare off, shut off the truck, and headed to the back of the trailer to unload her.

The door was already open.

Just like this.

My mare was in the first stall, held in place by the divider in my two-horse, slant-load trailer

"Did you open the door?" I asked my friend.

"No, did you?" she countered.

Nope.

The nut that bolted the door retention bar had rattled loose on the country roads, and the door opened.

While my worst trailer fear centers around a horse putting a foot through the floor, my husband constantly worries about this door-opening scenario. He hates having a horse in the back stall if there's an option to put them up further up, and he refuses to pull my trailer unless the horses are tied and the dividers are closed — all of which I did that day, and they are the reasons everyone is safe and sound.

I watch my mirrors like a hawk, especially while making turns, and while there was some traffic on the road no one indicated that anything was wrong. It was a small rural community, so I'm confident someone would have honked. My best guess is that the door mechanism finally gave way as I was pulling up the driveway.

I got lucky. If the weather had been nicer, I was going to bring two mares. If I had, one of them would have been in the back stall without a safety between them and the open door.

My fault was not recognizing that the trailer door didn't have a secondary latch as a fail-safe in case the primary one failed. Some trailers I have owned have had one, and some haven't, so I didn't think anything of it. The carabiner was an additional security for the primary latch, but it didn't count as a secondary.

Something as simple as a latch from a hardware store screwed onto the edge of the door could have prevented this from happening.

That kind of latch is definitely not appropriate as a primary door closure, but as an emergency back-up it would have (probably) kept the door closed until I had a chance to see that something was wrong.

Of course, using hindsight, the bolt and nut is being replaced with nylalock nut and bolt, and it's yet another maintenance item I will check regularly.

If the worst had happened and there had been a horse in the back stall, I use breakaway ties in my trailer. They won't release with normal jerks and pulls, but if a horse goes down, or falls out the back of the trailer, they will release and leave a tab on the halter. There's rarely a perfect solution to every potential accident that could befall a horse, but in most cases I think a breakaway tie in a trailer is a good idea. In my experience, baling twine breaks, or doesn't, unpredictably, and I prefer to use ties that are designed for this use. My ties have been tested a couple of times over the years and can be put back together and reused after releasing.

Endurance riders are hard on our trailers and vehicles, and we use them often. I think that's why more weird stuff happens to our horses and our equipment, even though I think that as a group endurance riders are educated and work hard to prevent bad things from happening. It's very difficult to put together a list of hard and fast rules that apply to everyone's individual situation to prevent every accident. In fact, by preventing one thing we could be increasing the risk of something else! However, I don't think it would hurt to take a look at how your trailer latches and evaluate whether a single point could fail and cause the door to open. Remember, it wasn't the latch, which was made extra secure by a clip, that failed. It was a single bolt and nut, which held the latch onto the trailer, that failed. If your trailer is similar, add a secondary safety latch or make that single fail-point a regular part of your trailer inspection.

Division of Labor

How it should work: *You have your job and I have mine.*

How it seems to work: *I'll do your job poorly and you do mine!*

Endurance Horses Got Skillz

I'M SURE EVERY affectionado of a particular horse sport has a pet peeve when it comes to how the horse's training is perceived by people in other horse sports. Dressage is more than being able to have three gaits and go in a circle, and jumping potential is measured in ways other than the frequency a horse jumps out of its paddock. It turns out that endurance horses are not badly-behaved trail horses that never learned how to stop.

I have tried my hand at all three of these sports, and while all three demand a performance horse, the skill set is vastly different for each.

Oh yes. Endurance horses have skillz.

Something that seems to escape not only the wack-a-doo putting "endurance horse potential" ads up on Craigs List, but also some people I consider experienced horseman.

Most of the time I laugh and shake my head, recognizing the inherent bias we all have when viewing something from the outside.

But once in a while, it really bugs me.

Not-so-recently I was reading something on well-behaved trail horses. The general gist was that unless you are planning on doing something endurance-like with your horse there is no reason to let your horse eat under saddle, and doing so will create a dangerous habit where the horse will learn it can rip your reins out of your hands and eat whatever choice morsel it sees on the trail.

Ummm, no. Just no.

Would you not teach your horse to canter because they will learn they can do it whenever they want? NO! You teach them that cantering is acceptable when you ask, and it is not OK to bolt through your hand and seat and do it whenever they want.

Do you not teach your horse to whoa from a trot or canter because that will lead to them stopping whenever they want? NO! You teach your horse a good whoa so that it can be done safely and on cue.

Eating grass under saddle is a behavior that can be taught to be done in a polite manner just like teaching a horse to canter nicely.

It is *not* OK for a horse to rip the reins out of my hands — even if it's an endurance horse.

We can discuss the merits of teaching a horse to eat under saddle, or not, but eating and rooting are separate issues, as are cantering and bolting. One is a vice — the other is a cued behavior.

What about horses being used for kids? Some might concede to my previous point, but then argue teaching a kid's horse to graze under saddle will be problematic.

Again, skills versus vices. Beginner kid horses are not normally schooled in the art of the walk-canter transition. This is a skill, not a vice, but not one that is desirable in most kiddie horses being used for walk-trot lessons. A horse that has this skill might still be a suitable mount if that walk-canter button isn't too sensitive. Same with eating under saddle. A pushy horse that takes advantage of a kid's inexperience to eat grass and rip reins out of hands is no more desirable than a horse that is looking for an excuse to canter, and who canters at the slightest touch of the heels or lean forward.

There is a difference between a skill and a vice. If you are making judgments about the horse athletes in different sports, it is wise to consider whether the behavior contributes to the success of that athlete. If the behavior is widespread and contributes to success within the sport, it is likely a skill not a vice. You may not choose to teach your horse that skill, or to reinforce that skill because of a variety of reasons, but that does not make it any less of a skill.

You can teach your horse to eat safely under saddle. It is your choice of whether you want to do so or not. Just like it is your choice if you want to school your horse in a canter, teach it to load in a trailer, jump, touch things with its nose on cue, or back up.

Eating while under saddle is not a "necessary evil" for endurance riders and their horses.

Why do so many people and horse combinations have trouble with grazing under saddle? In my experience, it's probably because of inconsistencies in the enforcement. It's much easier to be consistent about insisting on a nice canter transition. Getting a buck, or a not-so-nice transition is scary and we are really good at saying, "That is not happening again." A horse that's a little more pushy about getting a bite to eat isn't that scary, at least at first. However, with clear expectations and consistency, just like everything else you teach your horse, grazing under saddle is a non-issue.

Sometimes it's easier for the horseman, and especially kids, to be more consistent on the "no" than on the "yes," and in that case the horses know the expectation is no grazing. However, a consistent use of "yes" isn't necessarily wrong either.

What I Wish Riders Knew From the Vet Line

I WOULD BE hard-pressed to decide what I enjoyed more, vetting endurance rides or riding them. Both are hard work and long days, but are rewarding and come with lessons learned.

Oh yes, I learn as much from working the vet line all day as I do out on the trail.

Here are the things that Mel-the-Vet wants Mel-the-Rider to do differently at rides, or continue to avoid doing, based on what she's seen on this side of the line— and maybe there are some things that resonate with you too.

Leaving a good impression during the veterinary control judge check boils down to two really simple things. Trot well, and stand still for the rest

No, this doesn't come naturally to all horses, but consider it another Endurance Horse Got Skillz[8] moment, and do the homework.

---

8. *See previous chapter.*

What else can Mel-the-Rider do during the veterinary exam?

- Be calm. The best looking and behaved horses seem to have riders who are projecting calmness. Take a deep breath before stepping into line

- Be organized. It helps the calmness part.

- Trot in a straight line.[9] This makes a huge difference. I can't emphasize this enough. Before starting to run pick a point and run *straight* towards it. Don't change your mind half-way and take off at a tangent, or make some weird figure-eight. It's an out-and-*back*, not a racetrack oval. When you reach the other side turn the horse around and run straight *back* to the vet on the same line you went out on.

- If told to go to a certain point, such as a cone, go all the way to the cone. Due to space limitations in the vet areas the trot-out can be short in my area. It can be a real surprise to have to trot the full length of an official trot lane. Do it anyway.

- Don't let your horse rub on vet or scribe. It makes the horse look like an ass, its heart rate to go up, and makes it difficult to do a good exam. Having the horse rub on the rider is slightly better, but is still not ideal because of the last two things. This is my number one pet peeve with Farley,[10] the rubbing. She picks the vet line to do it in because she knows

---

9. *I go more into depth on the trot-out in a later chapter.*

10. *My first 100-mile horse, who was a fantastic all-around endurance horse.*

I'm likely to let it go because I don't want to make a fuss.

- Keep the horse's head facing straight ahead during the exam. The position of the head can affect some of the parameters and the vets are trying to be consistent. Bonus, if the horse's head is still and facing forward it also isn't rubbing.

- Have less stuff on the saddle (keep it simple![11]), or at least tie it down better for trot-outs. Having a crap ton of stuff bouncing around and off the horse isn't fun.

- Don't make excuses.

- Keep buddy horses out of the way. It's fine to have one around for moral support, but use common sense and keep it outside the vet box if possible.

- Have someone else trot the horse if Mel-the-Rider can't do it well due to stiffness, injury, etc. It really does make a difference on how the horse presents.

- If you see or hear lame steps while trotting the horse, *keep going* for the full trot-out. It may not be consistent, which is an important consideration on whether the horse is fit to continue in the competition, and the vet will be able to give better information of what might be going on.

- Don't haze, and don't let the crew haze the horse unless it's actually needed. Some organizations that do endurance

---

11. *More on this coming up in a later chapter.*

type competitions don't allow hazing of any kind. Make sure you understand your organization's rules. Even at a ride where a wave or a shout is allowed (such as AERC[12]), it's not like, as a vet, I'm deaf and blind to what you just did. It gets taken into account when I'm scoring the horse. A horse that is being hazed in the first couple steps of the trot-out is also more likely to do something unexpected that might get someone knocked over or stepped on.

- Yes, a young or inexperienced horse might need a pop on the rump with the lead line or reins to start the trot-out. Phase this out eventually. As a vet I've actually been hit, and had a lot of near misses with the buckles on the end of long reins because of riders doing this. If you are going to do this at least warn the vet and scribe to stand back. The trot area can be tight, and there's less room than you think to wave stuff around.

As I rider, when my horse gets poor scores at the vet check I figure it's inevitable that it's just going to get worse. I'm going to get pulled, and there's nothing I can do that's actually going to make a significant difference between this checkpoint and the next.

Actually, that is absolutely incorrect.

You can really have a horse that looks better at the next check. It won't always get worse!!!!!!

Your best chance at this magically occurring phenomenon is to SLOW THE &*^&%^*) DOWN.

---

12. *American Endurance Ride Conference.*

Yeah, I know you think you are taking it easy. And that your next loop will be slower, but the trick is to SLOW DOWN MORE. If everyone around you has slowed down and you are riding with the same pack (albeit slower), you probably haven't slowed down enough.

Sometimes that means you have to get off. Sometimes it means spending extra time in the hold. Sometimes it means spending extra time at every single cooling opportunity to help the horse manage heat better. Combine that with a slower pace on the trail, and that's probably "slow enough." It makes an amazing difference, and it's the number one thing I will remember when I'm on the other side of the line as a rider.

There are a couple more tidbits from Mel-the-Vet that Mel-the-Rider should remember.

- A lot of older horses are still going strong in this sport[13] (yay!). I'm not the only one trying to keep a late-teenage horse going.

- If a vet says, "You should stand for best condition," then do it if you can. Don't argue with them about weight and time. If they say it, they mean it.

- Vets have very limited information on loops, mileage, and ribbon colors especially if there are several distances with loops all out of camp, and everyone is at camp at once. Always ask a question to the person who is likely to give you the most accurate information. When it comes to the

---

13. *More on this later*

trail that's usually someone who is not the vet.

Now I just need to go and practice my trot-outs, and not let all this fly out of my brain when I take my stethoscope off and put my helmet on!

Trot-outs

THERE ARE TWO parts to a vet check, a static part when it's essential to keep the horse calm and still, and the trot-out.

For my first couple of seasons I focused on making sure my horses were good citizens during the standing part of the exam and completely ignored the trot-out.

After all, I regularly took my horses out running with me, and if they could maintain a polite jog behind me then we had the trot-out nailed right?

Nope.

The problem with the trot-out is that within 20 seconds there are two starts, two stops from a trot, with a minimum of direction from you that will interfere or distract from the horse's movement. All this while keeping the horse within view of the vet and traveling straight, and ideally at an optimal speed that will show off the horse well.

That's a LOT going on.

How big a deal is this, *really?*

Compare the two pictures below.

Picture 1

Picture 2

These pictures were taken about seven years apart with the same horse and rider pair. In both pictures the horse is sound and both vet checks ended with the same verdict — fit to continue. But in the first picture I used the logic that a horse that trots nicely behind me on a trail for a couple miles is a horse that is well prepared for a trot-out. The second picture demonstrates a rider and horse that have prepared and practiced for the trot-out at home.

Here are the components to a good trot-out so your pictures are like picture 2 from the beginning!

- **Teach the trot-out ahead of time and practice**. Seems like a big "duh," but just by doing a few sessions at home with consistent cues you avoid a horse that is both surprised and not sure what it's supposed to be doing. Confusion and surprise is evident in my horse's body language in picture 1. Look at her ears and leg. Everything about her is going "WHAAA????"

- **Position the horse** in a way that sets you up for success. Note in picture 2 how I'm off to the side at the level of her shoulder, and there's some distance (about 3 feet) between us. This avoids inadvertently applying backwards pressure and causing my horse to balk (see picture 1).

- **Don't tuck the horse behind you**. The vet can't see the horse well.

- **Have a cue.** Trot-outs are different from jogging along the trail. I use body language and verbal cues to let the horse know it's time to perform, and not just slog along behind me. Trot-outs are cued just like I can cue a canter, trot, walk, or halt from the saddle. To teach the cue at home you can utilize a dressage whip, lunge whip, or partner to reinforce the trot when you ask.

- **Don't make your horse look lame** by inadvertently pulling, yanking, or letting the lead rope excessively swing while you run.

- **Don't look back at your horse during the trot-out** or when cuing her to move forward. See picture 1 for how well that works. When teaching the trot-out at home this can be the hardest part. Using a long dressage whip or lunge whip that I can swing behind me while still looking forward and not turning behind me is essential.

- **Pick a gait and stick to it**. In non-gaited horses this is a trot. In a gaited horse it doesn't really matter, but it shouldn't be switching gaits in the middle of the trot-out.

- **Pick a speed that makes your horse look good.** Not too fast, not too slow. Experiment with different speeds at home. Have someone video you, or ask an experienced friend to watch trot-outs at different speeds.

- **Prepare for the stop**. It's just as important to coordinate the stop as it is the turn. I like to give a low verbal cue and jiggle the lead rope so we both stop in a coordinated fashion, rather than stumbling to a stop like drunken idiots.

- **Have a plan for the turn.** I tend to turn my horses away from me, but it isn't wrong to have them turn towards you either. I like turning away because it takes a bit more brain for my horse to execute it, and it pushes them off of me, helping to reinforce that during the trot-out I want them away from me. Try to come to a soft stop, and then calmly ask for a turn. It doesn't need to be a hard pivot, and you don't need to trot around the corner. Be aware that late in the ride, or on a long ride like a 100-mile, making the horse's muscles work harder by engaging them in a hard stop or pivot could cause a brief muscle cramp.

- **Set the horse up for the trot back too**. Just because you are halfway done doesn't mean you can get sloppy now!

- **Travel in a straight line.** Keep your head up and look forward. That is one of the biggest faults in picture 2. Look where you are going.

- **Prepare for the second stop,** facing the vet. Don't be surprised if the vet has moved to the side. It could be she wanted a different angle to view your trot-out or, more likely, she's used to horses blowing through their handlers cue for a stop and doesn't want to get run over. But that's why you have practiced! I use the same cues as the first stop.

- **Stand quietly** and wait for completion of the remainder of the exam. This is possibly the hardest part of the trot-out to remember to practice at home. At the conclusion of the trot-out practice, the horse should stand quietly for a couple of minutes, especially if trotting causes them to be a bit antsy and prone to dancing and swinging around.

Congratulations! You have a trot-out that doesn't make the vets furrow their brows and you get good looking pictures from the beginning!

Keep it Simple

WHEN I AM a control judge[14] at endurance rides, it is hard not to notice that the riders with the most simple tack set-ups without a million things hanging off of them, their horse, and their saddle are the most relaxed riders who seem to be enjoying the ride the most.

That was part of some key 100-mile advice I got prior to my first 100-mile ultra run from Jack M.

> "The biggest thing I see with first timers (and also one of the most difficult things to do): LIMIT YOUR GEAR!! You don't need the blue and green coat along with 3 pairs of shoes, etc! If you only bring one jacket, you won't spend time wondering if you chose the right one on the course! On top of that, you won't waste time playing with all the crap you absolutely had to have!! I know that having all that gear is a safety net, but walking the wire without a net will really help with your focus and execution!!"

Keeping it simple.

It feels like I wildly swing from one extreme to another. Being so

---

14. *Also known as "vetting rides."*

prepared and having just the right thing, even in the most unlikely of circumstances, and then bringing nothing and feeling free and focused on enjoying the trail without figuring out how to keep that one bag from rubbing the horse and banging into my knee — that's me!

Having done it both ways in running, riding, and also in life, here are my thoughts on the stuff we bring to all three.

Less is sometimes more. I don't have any definite answers of what you should or should not bring, and I don't offer any lists to help you decide between the essentials and not, but I can offer you some of the things I've learned in my experience and offer some thoughts on how to figure it out.

- Having lots of stuff with me is a distraction. From keeping it from rubbing and bouncing, to considering weight, to having to bring yet another piece of gear to carry all the stuff I am bringing, I find I am less focused on enjoying the event itself.

- The more stuff I have "just in case" the more work it is to keep it updated, not expired, and in good shape. This takes time away from actually running or riding.

- In most cases when "something happens" I could have handled it just as effectively without all the stuff.

- In rare cases "something happens" and it turns out nothing I brought really makes a difference.

- The more obstacles between me and getting out on the

trails, the less likely getting out on the trails will happen.

- It's OK to be uncomfortable.

- The more simple the system, the less failures it will have. Failures such as not having to stop and dismount in the middle of the trail to pick up yet something else that fell off my saddle out out of my pack.

- Less stuff can make it easier to focus on what is important in the sport — my relationship with the horse, the beautiful trails, perceived exertion, not missing ribbons, and biomechanics. My mental space is more clear when I'm running or riding and keeping it simple. Consider that endurance sport is a mental sport and mental energy is a finite resource.

- It's not all or nothing. It's OK to carry some emergency supplies. A jacket and a water filter. A phone and some ibuprofen. A hoofpick.

- Often times buying the right gear can eliminate carrying two or three other pieces of gear. I simplify my system whenever I can.

- When I buy a new piece of gear I consider getting rid of the old version. Even if the old version is just sitting there not hurting anything, it's still gear that has to be maintained, thought of, worried about, and stored. I was surprised how freeing it is to keep only the gear around that I was actively using. Most gear, retired by virtue of getting another updated piece of gear, can be easily replaced if it is needed in the future. Now I consider the cost of replacement if needed in the future versus the non-monetary cost of keeping it around.

Need some practical examples of what I've done?

- Limited my storage space on the saddle. I got rid of the cantle and pommel bags. I only use a flat velcro pouch that attaches to the breast collar. Sometimes I add a boot bag.

- Found a hydration system that is minimum fuss and well-organized, and then sold the ones that didn't work out.

- Got rid of riding tights I don't love.

- Got rid of ride and run event t-shirts that aren't perfect (I still have plenty!).

- Sold tack that hadn't been used in years and was sitting there collecting dust "just in case," and running shorts that sat in the back of the closet and never get used since they were my last resort because they don't really fit anymore. Perhaps designate ONE specific bin where "just in case" tack can live. Everything else gets sold or thrown away.

- Experimented with clothing layers and figured out that a quality base layer often eliminates an outer layer, and I stay comfortable without doing the jacket on-and-off dance.

- Threw away gear that was well-used, served its purpose, and in reality no one else is going to want because it was kinda gross and used-up, such as old helmets (did you know they have an expiration date?).

- Stopped looking at used tack classifieds and "Here's the Cool Stuff Coming Soon" lists unless there's a specific piece of gear I have in mind, or there's a specific problem I'm trying to solve. A good deal is so hard for me to resist, and that's how I ended up with WAY too much tack that I spent a lot of time trying to make sure wasn't getting ruined in containers, and digging through stuff to find a particular object. Guess what? Since I minimized five years ago, I've missed NOTHING.

- Separated out the things being kept for sentimental purposes. Instead I display it somewhere that is not my working tack storage area. Minx's[15] bit is kept at home and displayed on my wall. It's not kept with my other bits because I don't intend on using it again.

- Gave away those old running shoes. I have a sister who is a similar size and she uses them for mowing the lawn, walking, and sometimes running if they are shoes that still have some miles left in them. I've also given pairs to friends who are doing the great shoe hunt[16] and wanted to try a brand or model that I didn't like after putting 20-ish miles on the shoes. Win all around! If I didn't have those options I'd donate them to some program. But if they were seriously used? Trash 'em.

---

15. *My first endurance horse that died too young from colic at home (not ride associated).*

16. *Imagine having to replace your saddle every season and when you find the perfect saddle, it only exists for a few years until the manufacturer decides to update it. That is what it is like to buy shoes for ultra running.*

- Tried doing without it. I liked the security of a million buckets that I could theoretically put things in, but when I got rid of them *all* except two (one for each horse, and I chose my favorites), I loved not tripping over them in the tack room, finding mold in the bottoms, or keeping track of them even more than I liked having a million buckets.

- Added something to my trail kit only when there is a proven need. Like my miniature water filter straw. Twice I didn't bring it, and twice I really could have used it. Lesson learned. Twice in a race, I misjudged when I would come into an aid station and didn't have a light with me when I could have used it. Now I carry a small flashlight with me the whole time.

- Tried going out with nothing to see what happened.[17] I've done 10 mile runs without carrying food and water, and I ran longer races just relying on the aid stations. I didn't die, and I learned useful things.

- Simplified for events. I used my not-quite-as-good battery headlamp for my 100-mile ultra run instead of my nice rechargeable one because there was a LOT of darkness for a November 100-mile race, and switching out batteries on the fly was a lot simpler than coordinating headlamp swaps and recharges with the crew. It was fine and completely adequate. Likewise, I try really hard not to switch saddles or tack in the middle of endurance rides.

- Sometimes simple is a lot of work. More organization and

---

17. *Don't be a dumb-ass. Do this within reason.*

planning goes into my prep when I'm making things as simple as possible for an event. I package my food differently so at a vet check or aid station I can just grab a pre-made container. I go over (and over, and over) my gear thinking about all the possibilities and whether I've made the *best* single choice for the situation, such as a dry shirt and arm warmers instead of a jacket for the night portion of a 100-mile race. Evaluating need and throwing away stuff when it's time to purge my tack room is a lot of mental work for me. The pay-off is the mental calmness and focus I gain later on when I'm actually using my gear and doing epic things.

Taking the keep it simple philosophy seriously, simplifying my system, and getting rid of gear I don't use has absolutely increased the joy I feel while on the trail. Consider not packing the kitchen sink next time you head out.

Conditioning Plans

CAN YOU PLEASE give me a week-by-week plan of how to condition a horse for 25, 50, or 100 miles?

No, and here's why.

If you've been a reader here on this blog for long enough you know the chorus I keep repeating over and over and over. *It's important to understand the underlying mechanisms of how our endurance horses do what they do. Only then can you critically evaluate the methods, programs, and philosophy we apply to our horses and then interpret the results.*

Put another way, there are no cookie-cutter approaches for preparing an endurance horse.

What is left to us? An understanding of the fundamental science behind real-life training concepts and the ability to mix and match techniques to fit the individual horse and goals of the training.

It's not nearly as easy as printing a chart off the internet and following it week by week. Sorry.

When learning about the underlying concepts of endurance horse training it's useful to look at the running world.

I've said it a hundred times, and I'm going to say it again.

Horses are not the same as humans.

Humans are not the same as horses.

Did you hear me? Humans are not the same as horses.

Interpreting the exercise physiology between the two species has to be done with caution.

But that doesn't mean that it is an exercise in futility to do a bit of cross-species reference.

One of my favorite authors on running training is Steve Magness. In his book "Science of Running," he covers "Rules of Training," some of which are applicable to endurance horses.

Hype cycle. This is basically the concept that when some idea is new and popular, it gets overemphasized until it eventually falls into its rightful place. All sorts of things pop into mind such as electrolytes, BCAA's, interval training, barefoot.

Research is only as good as its measurement. Here's an excellent quote from Magness:

> *"We overemphasize the importance of what we can measure and what we already know, ignoring that which we cannot measure and know little about."*

Folks, that's our vet checks in a nutshell. The emphasis on heart-rate[18] (resting or recovery) springs to mind. The exact age a horse is put under saddle. What the magic numbers are for endurance horse longevity. There's a lot we don't know about endurance horses doing endurance. Some things we can easily see and measure, and as a result, we sometimes forget or ignore everything we don't know in favor of a flawed measurement that we are using only as an indicator for some process we can't see or measure. Does a naturally low resting heart-rate really correlate to better recoveries and performance? Is going above 10 mph during a ride really reducing the longevity of a horse's career? Black-and-white rules rarely exist in the real world.

We think in absolutes. We want everything to be an either/or instead of a spectrum. Like I've said here many times, if I think something is black-and-white, it's only because I don't know enough about the subject. Do you have an absolute opinion about an issue in endurance? Or about horses? Is it impossible for you to see the validity of the other side's opinion? I would encourage you to at least consider the gray areas of an issue. There are many hot topics on our sport, and they are hot topics for a reason. It's because they are nuanced and complicated subjects that deserve more than just a gut reaction. Taking the extreme view is seldom good in the short-term, and rarely correct in the long-term.

Everything works in cycles. Whether you are a ridecamp reader asking yourself, "Is it that time again when we talk about loose dogs, carrying side-arms, and LD vs endurance?" Or if you are an

---

18. *Heart-rate is a very important indicator and can be used to evaluate how a horse is handling exercise. However, my point is that we rely on heart rate because it's easily measured, and often we use it because we can't measure what we are really interested in.*

old-timer who has seen the pendulum swing from too must rest, too much conditioning, and back, everything works in cycles. There is likely nothing truly new, just rediscovery of things once done, and forgotten.

Evaluate our sport with these concepts in mind and I think we are primed to make better decisions for our horse, and for rider fitness and preparedness.

When I gave myself permission to break away from published running programs, and told myself that I knew how to get myself to a marathon better than the cookie-cutter 12-week program, it was the most freeing feeling in the world. I've never had as much fun running as the day I stopped following a program.

When I stopped training my horse according to the "shoulds" and instead gave myself permission to adapt my ride conditioning to whatever I thought my horse and I needed to reach our goals, I started to have a lot more fun at rides because my horse was performing better and having more fun too.

Time Versus Distance

DURING CONDITIONING RIDES do you ride for time or distance?

When I was training for marathons, before I got smart and realized I could do this from the back of a horse,[19] I followed a program that believed time spent hitting the road mattered more than the actual distance that you did. Jeff Galloway said that the mileage of 26.2 miles isn't hard — it's the four hours or so you spend on your feet moving. To condition for propelling yourself forward for that four hours on race day he suggested spending more effort getting the time in instead of focusing on the miles.

This worked well for me for several reasons. Before the days of cheap and readily available GPS my mileage during training was always a rough estimate; however, there was another reason I planned for time rather than distance. It was a huge mental boost. I planned my long runs for the time it should take to complete them. For example, 11 minute per mile pace wasn't unreasonable for a 10-15 mile run. If I needed a 10-mile run, I would plan a two-hour run. If I needed 15 miles, I knew I would be out there for three hours. In most cases it didn't matter whether I was running for time

---

19. *The blog post this is based on was obviously written before I decided running ultramarathons was a good idea.*

or distance because both got accomplished. However, if something went terribly wrong, I didn't worry that I was going too slow to get in the miles. I just knew I had to suck it up for X number of minutes. Somehow, it's easier to say, "I can walk for another hour and be done," than to say, "I have 5 more miles to go, and so that's one to six hours depending on whether I run it or crawl it." It gave me the freedom to not push past that margin of safety that kept me from getting hurt because I was running for time, not distance, and I could go as slow as I needed to get that time in without the pressure of getting the miles in.

Usually every third long run or so I would completely hit the wall and do significantly less miles than planned, but I still got the time in. It never hurt me, and my next long run always went well, but more importantly, my motivation remained high, and I didn't get mentally burnt out.

The other training philosophy I followed, once I had a few completions and I was interested in going faster was this: You train for speed, and you train for distance, but you don't combine the two until race day, i.e. I never ran a certain number of miles in a certain amount of time. I either did speed runs that had a specific time and repetitions associated with them, or I did long runs of a certain number of miles. Only on race day did I try to run X miles in X time.

Done improperly this can be a recipe for injury and disaster. You have to be darn sure that your speed and distance work is preparing you for your goal distance and time, and that your goal is reasonable considering your base and past history. I ran several races before the "Big One" as confidence boosters and reality checks. For example, if I was training for a marathon I would run a 10K or a half-marathon throughout my training program to see how close to my target I was, and how I felt at those distances at speed. Based on the results I would adjust my training program.

Humans and equines are very different species, and it is NOT a good idea to extrapolate too heavily from a human performance program to condition the endurance equine. However, I think there are several concepts in my running background that have helped me when preparing a horse for an endurance ride.

1.   Focus on time in the saddle rather than distance during a conditioning ride. Often the trail doesn't turn out to be as rideable as I'd thought, or weather makes the footing icky, or I need to work through some training issues, or the trail is too steep or rocky to go at an endurance pace. I may have an idea of the number of miles I would like to get in a particular ride, such as 15 or 20 miles, but I'll plan for a three to four-hour ride. I try to keep my speed at any moment below 10 mph at this stage. Focusing on time helps me to not push Farley or myself too fast or too far in a situation that is unrealistic to get in the miles in the time that I want.

2.   On shorter rides ("tune-up" rides) that usually happen around home that are usually 30-60 minutes long I do go endurance pace, or even a bit faster. If for example, if I'm working a dressage canter.

3.   At some point during the training, usually once she can go on a four-hour ride at a walk and trot on a decent trail that allows for a significant amount of trotting, I make an effort

to either set up a mock-LD at home, or we go to a real LD. Depending on her performance I adjust my training and my goals.

4.   During a ride, similar to the conditioning ride, I'm out there for a certain number of hours, whether that is six hours for an LD, 12 hours for a 50, etc. Whatever miles we accomplish in those hours depends on how rideable the trail is. If the trail conditions are really tough, we may come in overtime. What matters is the training and conditioning, not the completion.

Often the trails I see on official ride day can be ridden faster the trails I train on at home. It's important to remember not go too fast on race day if long training hours have been spent mostly at a walk and trot.

In my experience, two things can go wrong at a ride.

1.   Occasionally I go to a ride and realize I have an under-conditioned horse for the trail that we will need to do that weekend. This is usually because I've focused on miles in training rather than time in the saddle. I've chosen easier trails that can be done at an endurance pace because I'm concerned about getting the miles completed within the allotted time I have for training.

2.   When my horse gets injured at a ride or before a ride it's also because my training has focused on miles rather than time in the saddle. I tried to go faster on trails than was wise in order to try to get a certain amount of miles in a certain amount of time.

How to Condition

IN CONDITIONING FOR endurance, first you need to build a base. I actually think that endurance riders are really good about setting up a base for their horses. It's moving out of building base and moving onto the next stage that they seem stuck at, myself included.

Speed work and intervals have gotten a bad rap in both endurance and running. Is speed work only necessary for those people who want to go fast in races? NO. Done properly, speed work and intervals will put more fitness on your horse with less miles and is an important point of the three cornerstones in endurance training — rest, long rides, and speed. This is true even if, like me, your motto is "to finish is to win."[20]

When I create a conditioning program for a horse this is how I think about it.

Stage 1: Build base. This is the long, slow miles portion of the conditioning. At the end of the stage the horse looks good after going three to four hours at 5-7 mph. Completing an LD looking good is good indication you have completed Stage 1.

---

20. *Common motto in endurance riding.*

Stage 2: Add interval work and longer distance work. At this point you are still building fitness to the point where a horse can do a slow 50. Stage 2 doesn't look any different than Stage 1 except now you do the occasional four to five-hour conditioning ride (or LD), and about once a week you do faster work in the form of canter intervals or dedicated hill work.

Stage 3: Your horse has the fitness to do a slow 50-mile ride. Now you have a choice. Are you going to continue to build intensity and mileage into your routine for super-fit, or are you going to back off and just do the minimum to maintain fitness between rides for super-rested?

The biggest mistake I see is people staying in Stage 1 too long. You can only build up so much mileage. You aren't going to do a 50-mile training ride before your 50-mile endurance ride. At some point you have to incorporate other types of riding into your routine (Stage 2). The other big mistake is going directly into Stage 3 without spending any time in Stage 2, or going into Stage 3 without any conscious decision of which type of Stage 3 they want, ending up in the no-man's middle ground with a horse that is never quite fit enough or rested enough for them to reach their goals.

I like to visualize the choice between miles and recovery as a see-saw:

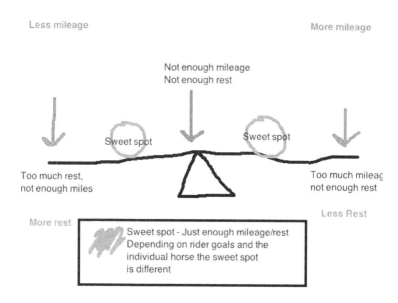

Both sweet spots can be successful. If you are trying to move up distance, to a 100-mile for example, you can use strategically placed 50-mile rides, conservative riding, and prudent ride scheduling to achieve that goal on the side of the see-saw that emphasizes rest. Alternatively you can focus on more mileage and conditioning, including cross training, to have a horse that is well-conditioned for the ride.

It varies for each horse, but here is what I would consider a super-rested and a super-fit protocol for a horse in Stage 3.

Super-fit protocol EXAMPLE

Long rides of about three to four hours, at speeds of at least 5 mph average every 7 to 14 days. Horse is ridden most days of the week, a mix of dressage schooling, shorter trail rides, and a fast ride of about one hour every 7 to 10 days. Reduce this workout in the last two weeks prior to a 50 or LD ride. This would mean the horse is still ridden three to four days a week and those rides include schooling dressage, and slower trail rides up to one hour. The two-week taper period would also apply to a 50-mile ride. For 100s the lead-up taper period prior to a ride is even longer than two weeks, approaching four weeks, with ideally no significant rides, such as a 50-mile, within six weeks of a 100-mile ride.

A super-fit protocol will give you the reserves to make-up time after situations such as getting stuck behind a long line of people, or a major tack malfunction.

Remember, resting the horse before a ride, and giving every other weekend off after doing significant long conditioning rides is essential for keeping the horse sound!

Super-rested protocol EXAMPLE

One or two long rides per month that are usually about three hours long. Ride horse about two days a week, and sometimes weeks go by without the horse being ridden. No more than one hard workout a week, whether that was a long ride or a faster interval ride. Even more typically "hard" workouts are spaced out by 10 to 14 days. You may cluster your workouts such as doing two or three harder, longer, or faster workouts back to back after 7 to 10 days off, followed by another 7 to 10 days off. Days off means fartin' around and doing rides without fitness goals. This includes fun rides with friends and beer, leadrope runs, ground work, swims in the lake, etc. If you have a time and a distance in mind it is not a day off.

A cornerstone of this approach is that you absolutely must make sure your horse is rested going into the ride, and you absolutely must make sure you don't put your horse back to work after a ride or an especially hard conditioning ride too soon. Wait weeks if necessary. Never ride your horse through being not-quite-right. Realize you are NOT going to beat that cut-off time by galloping five miles. The benefit of this approach? Going into the ride I'm not worried that there is something brewing somewhere.

Neither approach is without its risks. Super-fit? Look for stress injuries and micro injuries caused by fatigue. Tendons and ligaments are only as strong as the muscles around them, and fatigued muscles are asking for an increased load on a tendon that causes failure. Super-rested? If you have a horse with a history of tye-up[21] you must make sure you are addressing it through nutrition and how you are asking the horse to go back to work.

What about an approach that is in between these two options? I would argue that you have the risks without any of the benefits. You have a horse that you are riding a lot that may be more fatigued than optimal, but the type of work being done by the horse isn't adding to their fitness.

The bottom line is if you are happy with how the horse is finishing whatever is your choice of rides (LDs, 50s, 100s), then don't change anything. It doesn't matter exactly where you are on the see-saw because it is working for you. However, if you want the horse to look different at the finish line you must change something in your conditioning plan in order to change something in your horses fitness. You could be in the middle of the see-saw (not enough

---

21. *Exertional rhabdomyolysis*

mileage and not enough rest), or at the extreme ends of the see-saw (not enough mileage OR not enough rest). You either need to add rest or miles, and which option you choose will depend on your rider goals and your individual horse!

Here's another look at the diagram from above. At the arrows, the horse is too tired. At the circles the horse finishes well.

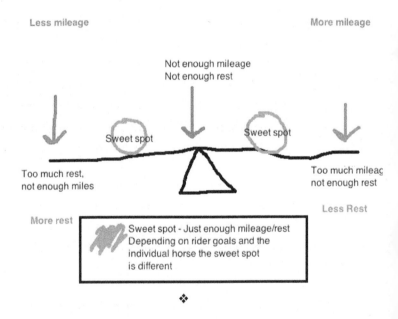

You can also look at this as a two-by-two diagram. (In vet school we get like a gazillion two-by-two diagrams to explain everything.)

	Lots of Miles	Less Miles
Lots of Rest	What reality are you in? Good luck making this combo happen.	Super-rested horse. High risk of acute fatigue injury, but doesn't have micro-injuries from training
Less Rest	Super-fit horse, higher risk of overtraining injury, but has the fitness to overcome the unexpected.	Not sure you are going to make it to a 30, 50, or 100...

Here's something else to think about:

What about injury? I've touched on it briefly above with stress and overtraining injuries associated with super-fit protocols, and more acute overriding injuries associated with super-rested protocols. Another thing to consider is a known history of some injury that you don't want to re-injure. An argument could be made for either philosophy.

Let's take tendons as an example. Assume you have successfully rehabbed the injury. It was a relatively mild injury that required time off, but wasn't necessarily career ending. The fact is: the previously injured tendon is not as strong. Tendons experiencing increased load have a tendency to protest. Tendons are kept in working order by the strength of the muscles around them. Tendons are susceptible to both overtraining and stress injuries, and overriding injuries. Keeping that in mind, here are some things to consider:

- Super-fit: You've thoroughly tested the tendon out on the trail and it hasn't broken yet, so you are probably OK to go. The downside: You've put a lot of stress on that tendon in training and it may have micro-injuries. In fact, the research says the tendons probably do. You are relying on the conditioning of the surrounding structures, such as the muscles, that may or may not have overtraining injuries or fatigue themselves.

- Super-rested: You've not overloaded the tendon in training, so you know you are going into the ride with as close to 100% integrity as it's ever going to have — the risk of some micro injury is low. The downside is the muscles around it may not be as adapted for the load, and thus the tendon may experience more strain during the ride and muscle fatigue during the ride may cause injury.

Again, there's a trade-off and a grey area of what exactly is the right approach. It goes back to the rider goals, the individual horse, and type of rides being selected.

Conditioning

WHEN I POST on this blog about how to condition the endurance horse, I'm painfully aware that it's largely based on my personal experiences with my horses, which is highly unscientific. Nothing more dangerous than some confident personal anecdotes right? Even if you adamantly disagree with some of my advice, that's OK. My hope is that even if you think I'm full of horse apples, there may be one little gem in there that you can take away and think about. That's certainly what I do when I read other people's stuff; I rarely agree with everything they say, but there's usually one thing I can take away.

Those of you who are long-time readers of this blog may read some of the stuff I posted yesterday[22] and say, "But that's not what you said three years ago!!!!" and you would be right. As much as I value consistency, I value having an open mind and constantly reassessing my methods to the best of the current knowledge out there even more. So yeah, my philosophy on conditioning has changed over the years.

Today's post is concentrated on my experience with conditioning an

---

22. "Yesterday's" post was published as the chapter before this one, "How to Condition".

Arabian versus a non-Arabian.

I'm going to start with Farley because I think it is easier to talk about Arabians and then contrast the non-Arabians. *Remember that this is my opinion in my one-rat study.*

After building a base on Farley I started doing 50s, and fairly quickly I attempted a 100.

Let's remind ourselves what my conditioning see-saw looks like:

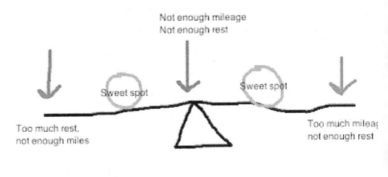

In the first part of Farley's career, up to the first time I attempted Tevis,[23] I operated in the sweet spot in the left side of the see-saw:

---

23. *A local 100-mile endurance race.*

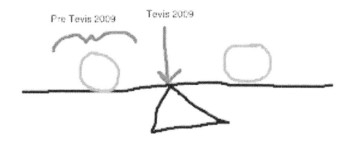

I stayed in this sweet spot for a year and accomplished a lot. But then, with Tevis on the horizon, I started to push. I started to move towards the right-hand side without really acknowledging it was happening. A major factor in my Tevis 2009 pull[24] was that I had shifted from one side of the see-saw to the other without *quite* making it. I needed either more rest or more mileage, and as a result I ended up in the uncomfortable position in the middle.

How do you know where you are on the see-saw? Hindsight is, unfortunately, a great instructor, but if you know you have minimal miles for what you are trying to accomplish you are on the left-hand side. If you are trying to make-up for those minimal miles by getting in one last ride before a race, or if you are pushing for your

---

24. *I only completed 65 miles of the 100-mile ride before being pulled from the race because of a lameness.*

horse to go harder and faster during those last rides because you
are stressed about the amount of conditioning, and they aren't
giving it to you, then it's very possible you are starting to move
towards the middle.

After Tevis 2009, I added dressage lessons, interval training, riding
more days out of the week, and more endurance rides to my
season. I moved to the right-hand side of the see-saw.

I stayed in that sweet spot for over a year and did more amazing
things! I did three 100s that year, including Tevis, and Farley
looked *great*. But then I added jumping to our cross-training and I
asked for one ride too many in the context of everything else we
were doing. This caused me to shift once again even further
towards the right-hand side of the see-saw out of the sweet spot,
and I got pulled again.

I want you to notice a pattern. First, I have two pulls,[25] one from each side of the see-saw. Choosing one philosophy over the other does not make you immune from getting pulled. Second, both my pulls resulted from me shifting to the right of the see-saw towards more miles and less rest, rather than the other way. Far more damaging than not enough miles is the effect of not enough rest.

The saying goes:[26] *It is better to show up under-trained and well-rested, than tired and on the brink of an injury.*

How does this relate to a non-Arabian?

In my experience, a non-Arabian, in general, needs more miles to achieve the same amount of fitness, and it needs more miles to maintain that fitness.

The rules of rest still apply, but somehow you need an increased number of miles while still maintaining enough rest.

Which means you are always operating in the shaded quadrants instead of one of the unshaded ones.

---

25. *It's now been many years since this post first appeared on the blog and I have even more pulls now! Most of them still relate more to over-riding than under-conditioning.*

26. *Yes, of COURSE you have to actually train. Take anything to the extreme and you have something stupid.*

	Lots of Miles	Less Miles
Lots of Rest	What reality are you in? Good luck making this combo happen.	Super-rested horse. High risk of acute fatigue injury, but doesn't have micro-injuries from training
Less Rest	Super-fit horse, higher risk of overtraining injury, but has the fitness to overcome the unexpected.	Not sure you are going to make it to a 30, 50, or 100...

I found that even with a LOT of miles I wasn't getting as much bang-for-my-buck, so while that number of miles would have put me in the super-fit category on an Arabian, it didn't with my Standardbred (non-Arabian). But, I needed more miles to keep her fit, which kept me out of the super-rested category.

Again, I'm fully aware I'm talking personal anecdotes. Your mileage may vary.

LD or 50?

HERE'S THIS WEEK'S question:

"I've noticed that a lot of serious endurance riders are skipping the LD's and starting their horses on 50s. Can we talk about the risks versus benefits of doing that? Assuming you're starting with a well-conditioned mature horse."

Assuming a well-conditioned mature horse I don't see any reason to start in an LD unless there are other mitigating factors. Some good reasons to start with LD's could include:

- Rider has a physical problem that prevents them from realistically finishing a 50.

- Horse has a history of some sort of issue that makes a 50-mile finish unlikely.

- Rider has no interest in doing longer rides such as 50s or 100s.

- Rider is new to the sport and has never done an endurance ride before.

In general, I think there is no reason to take your well-conditioned mature mount to an LD. LD's are great for young and not-well-conditioned mounts. They are great for I've-been-inside-all-winter-and-desperately-need-a-motivating-event. LD's have value, but they are not a necessary stepping stone towards a 50.

Don't misunderstand me — if you love LD's and *want* to do LDs then do them. Even on your mature and well-conditioned horse. But there is no specific reason you *have* to do an LD before doing a 50.

In fact, I think there are a couple of good reasons to skip the LD's if your goal is to eventually do longer distances such as 50s, or especially 100s.

We know that expectation plays a huge role in human athletic performance. I think it's reasonable to assume that our horses have some sort of self-regulation based on expectation too. I've seen it numerous times with my endurance mounts. They learn the distances. Along with figuring out how vet checks work and our expectations of them at rides, they are trying to figure out what their job is. Once I would do a distance two to three times the horse figured it out. They would stop asking the question of, "How far are we going?" and instead start asking, "How fast can I go?"

I didn't want my horses to stop asking the first question until the answer was "100 miles." The only way to keep them asking it was to not let them establish an expectation of an LD distance.

I think the benefits to skipping LD's and going straight to 50s, in a mature, well-conditioned mount, are:

- Establishing expectations and work ethic early

- Saving money

- Building confidence in yourself and your horse by riding a training LD at home. That is a great way to prepare for the rigors of an endurance ride regardless of the distance you are riding.

The potential risks?

- If you have misjudged your horse's physical or mental conditioning there is a higher risk of injury or burnout in a 50 than an LD.

I think a more experienced endurance rider is able to better judge the fitness and readiness of their mount, minimizing the risk, and this might explain why many of us choose to skip LD's.

Just One More

A BIG LESSON I've learned in endurance is the danger in asking for "just a little more."

The line between "fit enough to do get the distance done" and "over-conditioned and injured" can be very narrow indeed. When in doubt arrive to the ride well-rested and a little under-trained, instead of tired and on the brink of injury.

Bonk

NOTE FROM DR. Mel: A bonk is a bonk whether you are riding a horse or running. Although this post was inspired by a long run, it applies equally as well to riders.

I went for an awesome 20-mile run on Sunday with a friend and had the easiest, best, most-fabulous 20-mile training run EVER.

My friend, unfortunately, did not. In fact, she spent the last hour in a pretty serious bonk. After she started talking to me again (She probably spent the one-hour bonk silently swearing at me inside of her head. It's OK Jo, I didn't take it personally.), she told me I needed to write down my approach to fixing a bonk.

First off, for those of you not familiar with the term "bonk" here's a quick explanation. It can be physical, mental, or emotional. For example, any and all of these things could happen during a bonk:[27]

- GI distress, nausea

---

27. *These signs can also indicate a life-threatening condition such as heat illness. Make sure you are evaluating your entire situation, stop, and seek help if there's a possibility that a serious medical condition may be present.*

- Weird cramping pain in either GI, muscles, or connective tissues

- Dizzy

- Can't keep your eyes open

- Sudden tiredness, where before you were bouncy

- Feeling like it's impossible to take another step

- Hard time formulating sentences

- Crying

- Seriously thinking about choosing to DNF or rider-option[28]

Here's Mel's approach to the bonk.

First, recognize the bonk. How fast you can fix a bonk depends on how fast you can recognize yourself, or your friend, barreling towards it. A bonk that used to take you an hour to fix might be fixed in 15 minutes next time, or faster, if you recognize the subtle signs earlier. Here's what I look for.

Early signs that I'm bonking:

- When I'm talking to someone there's a two-second delay between me speaking and me hearing myself say the words. So far only happens to me at night.

---

28. *DNF stands for "did not finish," typically used in running races. Rider option is a type of pull in endurance that means the horse is fine but the rider chooses not to continue.*

- My mind is no longer active. It's hard to explain, but the constant background of my mind goes silent. It's not a pleasant "in the moment" type of silence, but a negative, dark emptiness.

- It's all I can do to get motivated to run a flat or downhill portion of the trail.

- I'm annoyed by my normally delightful friend or comrade.

- I use colors to designate run effort and assign the colors green, yellow, orange, and red to represent easiest to hardest efforts. Sections of trail that should be a green or yellow effort, taking into consideration the time of day and mileage, are an orange or red effort during a bonk.

Middle of full-on bonk

- Any upset stomach type symptoms

- Weird cramping or pain that comes on suddenly and sharply, especially if it's not at a site of any previous actual known injury.

- Dizzy

- Can't keep my eyes open, let-me-sleep-on-that-rock tired, which is usually an afternoon bonk thing.

- Whining

- If I let it go past this that's when I actually start getting nauseous, and I might have actual muscle cramps, like calf cramps.

Recognizing the bonk in other people

- One word answers or grunts when before they were chatterboxes.

- I've peed three or four times and they haven't peed at all.

- They are complaining of stomach cramps or nausea.

- They are needing breaks or need to hike where before they were bouncing happily along, and we have similar fitness levels.

- I haven't seen them eating anything in forever.

Second, ask yourself these questions:

1. When was the last time I peed?

2. When was the last time I ate real food, not Gu-like product, electrolyte drink, or gummies?

Commonly the answers are "Awhile," or, "I dunno." This, along with any signs in the previous section, increase the likelihood that what you are feeling is a bonk and not just normal fatigue.

Third, follow an algorithm.

Why have a structured plan? Because getting out of a bonk is the ONLY time I can't rely on feel to do what my body needs.

My body needs calories, or water, or electrolytes, or some

combination of these things.

What my body wants to do is...nothing.

My body's strategy is maybe if I ignore it, it will all go away and somehow get better? Yeah. Not very likely.

Here's the process I go through for correcting[29] a bonk.

Slow down.

I try not to stop. I can do that later if needed. Reduce the effort to a green or green-yellow even if that's a slow shuffle. I try to pick a pace where my brain isn't having to spend lots of effort forcing myself to go forward. I want my effort to be on easy autopilot while I figure this out.

Paradoxically, my nature is to start pushing HARDER in a bonk. I will be walking, but walking really fast, at the limit of my effort. The brain has told me, "Just get this done," and while that may be appropriate near the end of a long race, it isn't going to help me get through a bonk. This is an example of not being able to trust what your brain and body wants.

"It feels so inefficient," my friend moaned when I told her to slow down her charge up a hill when she was too queasy to eat. Just remember, going forward at any pace trumps stopping. And getting through a bonk and being able to run with an easy effort again trumps fast walking while feeling miserable and sick.

---

29. *This isn't medical advice. This isn't going to work for everyone. Don't be a dumb-ass.*

Check in with hydration and electrolytes first.

If it's been a while since you peed then spend more time here. If you suspect it's a fueling issue at least check in with your electrolytes and hydration. If this is out of whack it's difficult to get calories in.

Mel's process:

- I drink water until my stomach feels full and sorta sloshing. Then I pop one or two electrolyte capsules depending on conditions.

- Evaluate in five to 10 minutes. Do I feel better or worse or same?

If you are more likely to be dehydrated than electrolyte deficient, spend more time drinking water before going heavy on the electrolytes. However, if you aren't getting results and you feel the same after 15 or 20 minutes of drinking lots of water, or feel worse after five to 10 minutes, don't be afraid to pop electrolyte capsules.

When working through a bonk, it's helpful to keep an eye on your watch and set deadlines. Give X strategy a certain amount of time, and if it's not working move onto something else. With experience you will know what that X time is and when you usually respond to a strategy. For myself, if I increase my water consumption and don't feel better in five to 10 minutes then it's usually my electrolytes. If you've let yourself get further into a bonk, or don't have a lot of experience getting yourself through one, you may need 10 to 20 minutes to execute each step.

Overhydration and dehydration can feel very similar.[30] It's a scary thing to have to decide which needs correcting in the middle of a bonk with a fuzzy brain. Experience helps. I know I'm more likely to have an electrolyte issue than a water issue unless I'm at altitude, it's at the end of the day, and I have a headache. Then it's hydration I need to correct followed by electrolytes. If you've started drinking a lot of water and have been feeling progressively better, but now improvement has stalled, that's another sign you may need to pop some electrolytes. My preference is to choose an electrolyte capsule with ginger in it. That really helps prep my GI tract for the next step.

Eat real food

What do I mean by real food? Anything that isn't a gummy or a Gel-like product. I've had good luck using applesauce packets. You can try that if you need a liquid, sweet consistency with no chewing. Remove whatever seems to be the tastiest from your pack, or a friend's pack, or out of the pack of the person passing you.[31] Again, like all the other steps above your body probably doesn't want to eat. But remember, that's why we have these steps. Because if you listen to your body at this stage you won't do anything, or you'll do it half-ass and it's going to take forever to get out of this bonk.

Mel's process:

- Take one bite.

---

30. *A recent experience with a friend during a run highlighted that early signs of heat illness can also feel similar to these problems.*

31. *I'm mostly kidding about this one. Mostly.*

- Evaluate in five to 10 minutes.

- If you feel the same or better take another bite, but keep it at one bite. If you feel worse try a different food.

- If you still feel worse try rinsing your mouth with some sort of liquid that has sugar in it and then spit. If that doesn't work reevaluate your speed, hydration, and electrolytes. This is where I might start stopping and taking breaks if I've gotten this far and it's still getting worse.

- At some point instead of forcing a bite at timed intervals you will feel hungry before the five to 10 minute mark. Feel free to eat according to how you feel at that point, but make sure to take at least one bite every 20 minutes.

Hopefully, at this point you have to pee if that was one of your "dunno" questions. I don't wait until I pee, if I haven't peed, to start eating, but I keep an eye on it.

Pick up the pace:

It's important not to do too much too fast. I usually don't force myself to run again, but while I'm eating I usually find myself wanting to pick up the pace. It's not a desperate push like when I first bonk, but an honest "I want to take a couple of running steps on this very runnable section." I choose strict end-points for these running stretches until I completely forget to stop at my end-point because my mind has wandered and the pace is easy again. I either count strides— 20 works well for me, or I choose a physical landmark. If there happens to be a nice down-hill I'll shuffle down it faster than a walk, but not a true run. During this time I'm still drinking, electrolyting, and eating. Usually by now any weird bonk pains in muscles or tissues have disappeared. The pace should still feel easy even though you're going faster than when you first identified the bonk.

Taken care of your internal governor.

Our brain has a huge role in how we feel as we cover the miles. It allocates your body's resources as it sees fit and makes you feel different things independent of what subjective reality is. If you have taken care of any pacing, water, electrolyte, and food issues and still find yourself dragging along, do a little brain self-care. I also try to do regular internal governor checks outside of a bonk.

Here are my favorites:

- Suck on Mentos or some other favorite delicious thing.

- Change up whatever I'm listening to. I switch between silence, podcasts, and music.

- Pull out the map and calculate likely time to the aid station and see how close I can come to the second of being there, or try to beat my estimated time.

- Do walk-run intervals based on landmarks.

- Make an aid station plan. What am I going to do, and what am I going to eat?

- Play games with the distance. I only have to get to the next aid station; the rest of the distance doesn't exist.

- Help someone else out on the trail who's having a tough time.

- Take some pictures.

Other helpful hints and tips:

- Getting through these steps during a bonk is so hard that it often takes a constant dialogue from a friend or self-talk to remain focused keep and doing them. It sounds so stupid as I sit on the couch and write it out because it really is simple, but during a bonk *you are stupid.*

- The most important thing is not to copy my bonk system point-for-point. The most important thing is that YOU HAVE A SYSTEM for working through your personal bonks. You can't do nothing. You can't wait 30-60 minutes and then try one thing, and then wait another 30 to 60 minutes and sorta try something else.

- Sometimes there is a point where your body is under so much stress that you have to go to extremes to get back on track. I remember seeing my Western States runner puke at an aid station in the early evening after eating and being grilled by an EMT present about what he had been eating and drinking up until that point. He was told to have no more sugar, no more sugary drinks, lay off the solids for a while, and try to stick to chicken broth. After a couple of hours of chicken broth, things finally settled down, and he was able to start his normal refueling again. If nothing is working that usually works, and you can't trust what your body wants because it's obviously lying then trust the most trustworthy person around you. An EMT at a Western States Run aid station is a good choice! A more experienced runner or endurance rider is also a good choice as is your crew who has helped you through this in the past.

- Often just getting to an aid station and getting caught up in the excitement and thanking the volunteers, eating the yummy food, and executing your aid station plan is enough of a distraction and a boost that on the other side of the aid station you accidentally find yourself running again. This happens more frequently when I'm dealing with an internal governor issue, and my hydration and fueling is adequate, but I'm just struggling mentally.

- A common negative thought during a bonk is that you may as well give up because obviously it's never going to get better. That's a LIE. You cannot predict how you will exit a bonk. Sometimes the smoothest, easiest running is on the other side of a bonk. I've had some of my best running miles at 60 miles into a race which is CRAZY. How should running at the 60-mile point be easier than the 20? Trust in your body, and trust in the process.

- My preference is to handle my water, electrolytes, and the bulk of my calories separately. That allows me to micro-manage and balance them. I do have a few all-in-one products that I use as part of an overall fueling strategy. But if I'm using those products, I'm also carrying plain water and electrolyte tabs. I've heard some people swear by all-in-one products and say they don't need anything else, even for really long races like 50-milers. However, in my personal experience, I've seen friends and others around me bonk harder and more often using these products. Experiment. If you are regularly bonking and bonking hard try something else.

* The further I'm into a run or race the faster a bonk can progress from "mmm, maybe there's a problem," to full on "whoa baby!"

* I always tell people who are nauseous and trying to puke that they will feel better if they puke. I have no actual experience, but it's what I've always been told.[32] Getting nauseous is really late-stage bonk for me, and I rarely get to that point. But I've walked a ton of people through bonking nausea and they all told me how it helped, so I continue to say it.

---

32. *If you don't feel better after puking, it may be heat illness. That was the case for a friend on an August run. Always reassess and make sure a more serious issue isn't driving your symptoms.*

Imposter Syndrome

I HAD NEVER heard about imposter syndrome until I got to vet school. Apparently it's really common among vet students, even as you graduate and beyond, and it spilled over to my endurance life too.

It's a feeling that you aren't really good enough to be there. That any moment someone is going to find out you are a total fraud, de-mask you and exile you to the fringes as you deserve. It's not necessarily low self-esteem, or even a well-developed sense of humility. It goes along with the other spectrum of traits that the vet school application process seems to select for, as well as many people who are in the endurance sport — type-A, anxious, relatively introverted, and driven.

Off and on I have lesser or greater degrees of this feeling. I don't have a problem taking credit for my accomplishments. Now is the time to point out I have a BLOG that is DEVOTED to things I do and I accomplish. However, I have a strong sense that the accomplishments have a shelf-life, and then they are to be set aside. You are not defined by your past, only what you are currently doing and planning to do.

For example, on average, three or four days after receiving some memento celebrating an endurance accomplishment, I will start calculating how many days until I need to take it down and hide it away in the big container in the garage with the rest of my trophies.

About the same time, I will start using the words "fraud," "failure," and "former" in conversations again with friends. Jokingly, but also seriously. Why am I a failure? I haven't been on a run for four days. I feel like I study a lot less than other people in my class for upcoming tests. My endurance horse hasn't been ridden in a week.

During one episode my friends told me something I really needed to hear.

I need to banish those three "F" words from my vocabulary. I am none of these.

I was told to leave my race and ride mementos up for the season and not take them down because obviously I need visual reminders.

They were appalled when I told them I didn't have a single completion award or ride picture displayed in my house or office.

We talked about ride and run t-shirts, and I realized that when I'm having a bad week I wear a lot of ride and run shirts. Subconsciously I know they make me feel better and more confident.

It's impossible to feel like a former endurance rider when you are wearing the t-shirt you earned at that 50-miler two months ago.

So I made some changes.

I dug up my awards for the past year, both endurance and running related. I hung them somewhere visible and kept them there until the end of the year. That silly little medal I got for the 35K that I didn't feel like I deserved at the time? It makes me feel happy and content now that I'm not in a rush to take it down.

The Tevis Cougar Rock pictures that I got enlarged came out of their rolled storage in the closet, and I bought frames and mattes and put one in my office and one in my living room.

When I got the AERC yearbook in the mail, and Farley was listed for her 1000-mile accomplishment, I took a picture of it, and Facebook shared it.

Wanna know a secret? It was a lot of fun to add visible reminders of the things I am most proud of back into my daily life. A lot more fun then systematically removing them from sight as soon as I could bear it.

As for the "F" words? I haven't used them since. Not even jokingly. And when I do find myself wanting to fall into the routine I can look up and see a ride photo or touch my medals and feel proud of what I've accomplished.

Non-Arabian Endurance

I'VE WANTED TO write this post for a very, very long time. How long? Years.

It finally took a friend privately asking me about the subject to finally put my thoughts on paper.

Why the hesitation?

- Because my experience is the experience of one person and I don't want to discourage anyone.

- Because even though I know what I experienced and have watched others go through similar situations, I still believe in the power of determination and hope and a little luck.

- Because I still believe myself when I tell greenbeans[33] that YES, you can do this sport on a non-Arabian.

- Because I'm afraid of offending you, My Dear Reader, because if I don't explain myself well enough then

---

33. *A term that has been adopted in the last couple of years for people and horses just starting in the sport of endurance.*

you might think I don't support or believe in you as you go through your own endurance journey on a non-Arabian.

Here's what I learned doing endurance on a non-Arabian. Keep in mind that this is a one-rat study and my opinions and experiences may not be true for your specific circumstance.

I started this sport with a horse that was an off-the-track Standardbred that was very Thoroughbred-y and Arab-y looking. I say that so you can picture her. She wasn't one of those massive thick Standardbreds you usually see. She was 16-hands but all leg and slab-sided, and she was probably closer to 900 pounds than 1000. This is why even though I'm short I didn't look small on her. Overall she resembled a very large Arabian, except not as round.

She was very errr...athletic[34] and raced on the trotting track. She never won, but she loved the sport of endurance. She was in fantastic condition. In the beginning I had problems keeping her sound because of newbie endurance rider errors. But once I got the soundness problems managed,[35] and I started actually completing 50s, she was still extremely difficult to manage through 50s. She didn't effortlessly sail through the distance like I saw so many around me do.

---

34. *Yes, by "athletic" I mean that she also regularly dumped me because she was QUICK and had the MOVES. Not a mean horse - but one who built up ENERGY and nerves unless she got out most days and her default signature move could dump me faster than I could blink.*

35. *Keeping her sound was a dicey thing. "Managed" meant that it was no longer the limiting factor to completing endurance rides. With the benefit of some experience, she probably needed her hocks injected, and pasture turn-out so she could blow off steam without me having to ride as many miles.*

I used to think it was some failure on my part. I just needed to get better at various aspects of endurance, and then Minx too could get through 50s and endurance rides as easily as the horses around us did. The truth was that there is a reason most/all/vast majority of the top horses are Arabians or Arabian crosses.

Fifties that had other challenges added on beyond just the distance were not our friend. This included my final endurance ride on her, a hilly and hot 50-mile ride, which I rider-optioned at the lunch check even though she passed the vet check.

This was in spite of honing my electrolyte protocol down to a science in order to get her through previous 50s, and riding a smart ride that took into consideration all I had learned in the past two years conditioning her and while riding her in endurance rides. It was one of my better executed rides.

The only 50s we successfully completed were relatively easy 50s that were early in the season, and cool or rainy.

Even on those easier 50s that we did finish I felt that metabolically she was barely squeaking by, even though everything would look OK at the final vet check.

"Metabolics" goes beyond heat conditioning, heat dispersion, muscle strength, aerobic fitness, blood volume, electrolyte handling, etc. I believe we only know a fraction of the science of what it takes to get horses through an endurance ride, and I don't think we fully understand why some breeds[36] are good at the endurance thing and

---

36. *Please don't give me any of the lore of why Arabians are so much better at this than other breeds that is floating around like, "Their spleens are bigger!" In fact,*

some aren't. Minx was talented, fit, and loved endurance, but simply did not have the metabolics of an Arabian. Every 50 I did on that horse was far tougher than any 100 I've done on Farley.[37]

I thought if I rode in the middle or back of the pack, crossed my T's and dotted my I's then I would be consistently rewarded with completions with a horse that reflected all the work and research I did. If I didn't get completions or have a good horse at the end, I thought by doing more work I could fix it and make it better.

What I learned is that while I could be successful at easier 50s, there was a very good likelihood I would never be successful at longer or harder rides except through true luck with that particular horse. Too many things had to be perfect, and as we all know, rarely does luck and proper planning come together for perfect. Or am I the only one where it seems I have one or the other but never both in the right direction at any particular ride?

---

their spleens are smaller than other race-type breeds like Thoroughbreds and Standardbreds proportional to their size. The fact they "came from the desert" doesn't mean much to me. It doesn't tell me WHY they better, if indeed this fact is even related. Honestly, the whole concept reminds me of mustangs, which lose whatever advantage nature gave them after enough time in captivity. Not to mention, like many of our Arabians, mine did NOT come from the desert, they came from the foggy, cool coast of California and seem to do fine.

37. An Arabian mare that was my main endurance horse when I wrote this post originally. When I was contemplating doing my first 100 on Farley I was asked by another endurance rider whether I was sure I could tell the difference between my horse being honestly "done" or if they just needed a breather and would be good to go. I just laughed. Managing that line was ALL I did for the three years I owned Minx. Sometimes successfully and sometimes not.

Endurance is harder on a non-Arabian. There is less lee-way for mistakes, and you need a little more luck. It's why for my subsequent endurance horses, as much as I love certain non-Arabian breeds, I've never seriously considered getting another non-Arabian for this sport.

There is a justifiable pride and sense of real accomplishment that comes with doing this sport on a non-Arabian, but after two seasons with Minx, I was at the point where I *just wanted this sport that I spent so much time, money, and energy on to be fun.* I wanted more completions than non-completions, and my chances are a lot better with an Arabian than a non-Arabian.

Looking back, I don't have a lot of advice for my past self.

The biggest thing I would change? Choosing my rides more carefully. There are lots of endurance rides that are very local to me. Unfortunately, they represent some of the tougher rides in the region. Instead of being sucked into convenience, I wish I had sought out rides from the very start that were suitable and doable for Minx.

With the benefit of my current experience I do think I could have done a better job with Minx, just like I'll do a better job with MerryLegs[38] than I did with Farley. But beyond keeping Minx sounder and fatter (she wasn't an easy horse to keep weight on, but now I have some tricks!), I'm not sure I could have done a better job with conditioning programs, electrolyte protocols, etc. I suspect the outcome would have been the same — the easiest rides in my region, some LD's, and a career as my pleasure-driving horse — but

---

38. *The Arabian mare that came after Farley.*

maybe that realization would have been less traumatic for us both.

In a nutshell, if I were doing this sport on another non-Arabian, I would start with rides that play to that particular horse's strengths. The emphasis would be to keep it fun for them and me and see where it goes, and not pour my hopes and dreams into them like I did Minx.

In my experience, broaching the subject of how different the sport of riding 50 or a 100 miles is on a non-Arabian in a public forum quickly degenerates into people pointing to successful non-Arabian individuals that have done well, and everyone agreeing on the safe concept that yes, you can do endurance on any breed — as long as the individual horse is suitable.

The dirty little secret is that, at least from my observations, there are a lot more unsuitable non-Arabians than Arabians.

One reason the subject is difficult is because the examples we see around us are mostly the success stories, the Arabians and non-Arabians that have gone on to success in this sport. Non-successful horses are often a blip as they appear in someone's ride story and then quietly disappear, or are not written about at all.

For example a friend's Tennessee Walking mare is one of only a handful of Tennessee Walkers that have ever completed a 100-mile ride. Yet there are LOTS of stories and posts about people trying to do endurance on that breed if you look at facebook groups, email lists, and breed groups, etc. What this means is that most people who try to do 100s on a Tennessee Walker fail.

I'm not saying that your particular non-Arabian horse is like Minx, or that you can never be successful with a non-Arabian. But realize that your success or failure is not always a reflection of your preparedness. I've chosen to hedge my bets and ride Arabians for now. Whatever you decide, best of luck, and know that I'll be rooting for you.

Unfinished Business

SOMETIME IN HIGH school, I believe, I started working on a cross-stitch project.

A LONG time later (maybe 15 years or so?) this is what it looked like:

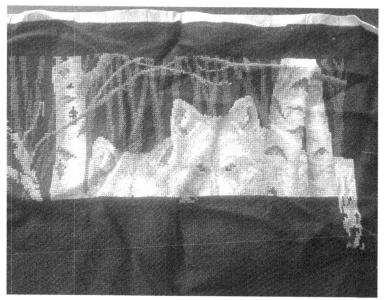

Half-finished, even though there were some concentrated, big, and sporadic pushes over the years.

With national veterinary boards behind me and more downtime on my hands I've been pulling out old half-finished projects and giving them another go. I was bored of knitting having made a zillion baby socks for a friend, so I settled into my recliner determined to get some significant progress done on this thing.

Twenty stitches later I had an epiphany.

I got exactly zero enjoyment working on this project with the blah grays and browns. It was tedious. I had been gritting my teeth for fifteen years trying to get this project done. The juxtaposition against the recent countless, satisfying hours of knitting was striking.

My first instinct was to grit my teeth and just do it.

After all, I finish what I start.

Or, at least I used to.

I've changed in the 15 years since I started this. Now I don't always finish what I don't enjoy. Sometimes I quit. Sometimes I ignore all the work, time, and money that has gone into something and cut my losses and say good-bye.

"Fine!" the little voice in my brain said. *"Put it away, and maybe later you will be in the right mood..."*

NO!!!!!!

I squashed that little voice with the biggest hammer I could find and made a decision.

Life is too short. The cross-stitch had to go.

Should I use it as target practice?

The more mature side of me (yes, I have one occasionally) offered it to my artsy-crafty sister in case she wanted to try her hand at it.

Giving up on an unfinished project is hard, whether it's a horse or a cross-stitch project.

When do you call it quits? When do you work through it because it makes you a better, more humble person? When is it YOU and not the horse?

Is it time for a change?

Often I see horse and rider mismatches that have a simple solution. Break up, cut your losses, and let both of you move on.

I always hope I'm making the right decision when I buy or lease or a horse, but sometimes it's not a good fit. Life is short and not every horse I touch deserves a forever home with me. It's presumptuous to think that I am the only person who can truly give a horse a good home. Sure, bad things happen, but that's true in life. You can't totally protect your kids, your horses, or your friends from it. But that doesn't mean you let your fear of what could happen to the horse keep you from moving that horse down the road where they could have a job they love, with a person they trust if they aren't getting that from you.

I feel that too often guilt or a sense that something bad might happen keeps people from making good decisions with a horse that isn't working out. This is different from an older horse near retirement being dumped because it can no longer perform of course, but I think too often people confuse the two issues and think they are one and the same.

Finding a home for a young, sound, healthy horse that isn't working out is the smart thing to do. Hopefully it finds a place in the world so it can then settle into a well-earned and deserved retirement some day. Wasting time on an obviously unsuitable horse while it is still competitively sound only wastes precious time for it. It could be finding its forever home. Before you know it, you have a late-teens horse that is still unsuitable for your home for whatever reasons, but now it has age issues and should be retired or lightly used, and it has lost that chance to find that right home.

We often applaud the tenacity of people who hold on and give the horse lots of chances, but rarely do we give the better advice of "move on."

But is the problem really you, not the horse?

We've all seen the scenario. Horse is bought. Horse is ridden. Horse develops exactly the same issues as the person's last horse. Horse is sold. Horse is bought. Repeat ad-nauseum.

I won't try to break the news gently, the root issue is you.

Or perhaps you are inherently attracted to the "bad boy" and simply cannot resist the pull of temptation. Only to have it later tempered by buyer's regret.

STOP DOING THAT.

Here's the irony of the situation. Those riders who should move on tend to keep horses. Those riders who should keep tend to move on to a new horse.

As anyone who has spent any time on the social media boards knows, *"Although the story of people ditching their horse and getting a new one is extremely common, the story of people ditching their horse, getting a new one, then having everything work out perfectly is very rare."* ~ Dressage Curmudgeon [39]

Whether some quirk or dark hole of unrealized ignorance of the rider is creating the same issue over and over, or the rider is simply attracted to unsuitable mounts the fix is the same — self-reflection and outside help.

I think that it is very difficult for you to determine by yourself which category you fall into, move on or stick with it.

Unfinished projects are tricky. A life full of horses and riding will probably have horses and issues that fall into both categories.

What do you do when you find yourself with an unsuitable mount, and you've determined that the circumstance fits into one or both of the above categories?

The end choices are the same: sell and buy appropriately, or keep and rehab.

The success and quality of horses in my life depends on making the right choice at the right time. Honest, truthful friends who know you and your horse can be invaluable. I am lucky enough to have

---

39. *http://dressagecurmudgeon.blogspot.com/2014_12_01_archive.html*

(finally!) a small group of friends in endurance whom I trust well enough to hear what I don't want to hear, when they say it.

I've been extremely fortunate so far in my endurance journey not have to make the hard choice of re-homing a horse. Horses that I realized did not make good partners for me were fortunately here on only a temporary basis. But if I stick with this long enough— and I plan on it, that will eventually happen. When it does, I hope I can make a decision unclouded by pride, guilt, and a need to finish a project "just because."

Of Widows and Boots

I HAVE A problem.

There's a black widow in my hiking-style, lace-up riding shoes.

I know this because like any good country girl I don't put my hands, or feet, in places that I can't see. And I saw it. Its fat shiny body. Before it crawled back into the toe of my boot.

Even in the absence of their very distinctive webs, if it looks like a likely habitat for black widows, such as wood piles and unused equipment, I assume that there is a black widow there until proven otherwise.

In equipment that IS used regularly, I don't generally worry about the widows, except if I see or feel a web. Then I go hunting...

Here's how it went.

I decided to do some dressage. There were visible webs on my synthetic dressage saddle, so I did a widow check. Didn't find anything. I felt that I got a good look in all the nooks and crannies and was able to get sunshine into most dark places, so I felt comfortable using the saddle.

I checked my boots like I always do for wasps or other critters that have decided to take up residence and saw... webs.

Crap.

Have you ever tried to see all the way into the toe of a boot?

I shook a dead wasp out of the bottom.

Maybe there wasn't actually a widow in there, and like the saddle, it was just webs?

Then I turned the boot towards the light and SAW IT— fat shiny body!!!!

AAAKKKKK!!!!!!

BAM! BAM! BAM! I slammed the boot against the ground.

To no one's surprise, including my own, no black widow fell onto the ground.

But now I knew it was there.

My barn owner came over. She declared that there was no black widow (But I saw it!!!!).

My boyfriend unlaced my boot, which by the way, cannot be laced up again because the laces are frayed, and stuck his hand in, quickly, and declared it widow free (But I saw it.....).

Here's a dirty little secret. This all happened two weeks ago. It's been two weeks. I haven't worn the boot since. My options are not good.

1. The widow is still in there and when I stick my, usually sock-less, foot into the boot, it bites me and seriously freaks me out.

2. I somehow squish the widow in the boot, and my foot comes into contact with squished widow. And seriously freaks me out.

3. I take apart my boot, find the widow, remove it with a stick and squish it. I then have pieces of leather that used to resemble a boot laying on the ground.

I cannot think of a way to GUARANTEE that there isn't a widow, dead or otherwise in the toe of that boot. And I saw it. I'm not making it up.

I am NOT sticking my foot into that boot without a guarantee of a widow-less environment in that toe.

I MIGHT be willing to stick a shop vac into the boot tomorrow and then declare it safe for toes. We shall see.

Anyone want to buy a pair of size 7 1/2 Ariat Terrains? One boot missing a lace.

Older Horses

EARLIER I SHARED some data that Mike Maul posted on the AERC facebook page. Now, instead of relying on your *squirrel-shiny-object-syndrome brains to go look at what I posted earlier and then come back here in a sort of orderly and reliable fashion (this is the modern age after all), I'll just reiterate everything here.

Oh, maybe that's just me? So says the blogger who felt the need to perfect a maple syrup and cinnamon roasted almond recipe prior to actually settling down and writing this post.

Here's what he posted:

Mike Maul ▶ AERC: American Endurance Ride Conference
3 hrs · 🌐

I was completing a data request today and thought the results might be of interest here too. It's the age... Continue Reading

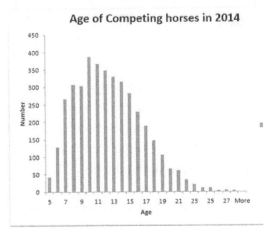

Age of Competing horses in 2014

Mike Maul
Here's the age distribution in 2004

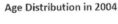

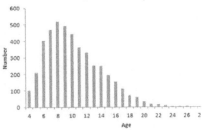

2 hours ago · Like · 👍 4 · Reply

Unrelated to this post, but worth mentioning, are the differences on the young horse side of the graph. Over the years there have been some changes in the age requirements for horses starting various endurance distances, which probably explains the drop-off in 4-year-olds competing. Now, back to the interesting part.

My initial impressions were that on the surface it looks like the mode of endurance horse age has shifted "older" about three years, from around 8-years-old to around 11-years-old. The mean (average) is probably even a couple years above those numbers, which means right now your average endurance horse is in its early teens.

As someone with a horse that's staring late teens in the face, who shows no signs of slowing down, I'm very interested in the right-hand side of the graph.

It's still a fact that in both 2004 and 2014 a horse in its late teens or 20s makes up a very small part of the population. I can't tell from this data whether that is because most of these horses are started in the sport in the 8 to 11-year-old range, and that's just a really long time to stay accident-free and genetically lucky, or whether it represents a few folks brave enough to start their older horses in the sport, and these horses are relative newcomers. It would be really interesting to look at each age group and see what their average number of previous seasons was.

So I asked for a favor.

Mike very graciously ran a database query and sent me the data for all horses finishing rides in 2004 and 2014, their ages at that time, and how many seasons they had completed to date.

Unfortunately the 2004 data wasn't usable. But even though we can't compare how the career of an older horse may have changed in the last 10 years, just looking at 2014 was interesting.

Some notes about the data before we get started

- A "season" means at least one ride completed, which includes LD's and seasons with only LD miles.

- The number of seasons can be non-consecutive and is cumulative.

- This is the biggest irregularity in the data: Ages of horses are as of 2014. HOWEVER, if that horse had completed a ride in 2015, then 2015 was counted as part of that horse's cumulative seasons under their 2014 age. This is why there are 5-year-olds in this data set with three seasons completed. A 2013 season as a 4-year-old, a 2014 season as a 5-year-old, and at least one ride completed already in the 2015 season as a 6-year-old, but counted as a 5-year-old in the graphs, etc.

- I spot-checked the outliers in the data just to make sure there wasn't funky going on. This is where the 2004 data failed the test and how I found out about the 5-year-olds in the previous bullet point. That 25-year-old horse with 21 seasons? That's Remington. The 25-year-old with 20 seasons? Robin Hood. Not errors, actual horses with impressive records.

Everyone likes a good graph, so let's start there, even though I think a graph in this case is actually less helpful then looking at the pattern of the raw numbers in the data table.

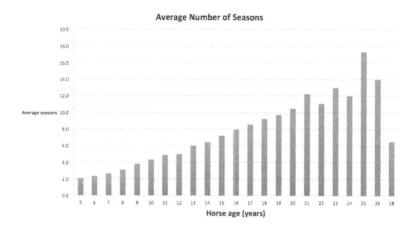

The older horses in our sport are not newcomers. That relatively small population of individuals on the right hand side of Mike's graphs are very experienced endurance horses.

More compelling is looking at the data in this format:

# of horses / # Seasons completed	5	6	7	8	9	10	11	12	13	14	15	16	17	18	19	20	21	22	23	24	25	26	28	Grand Total
1	4	19	10	13	7	9	9	7	7	4	4		3	3										99
2	5	40	66	40	31	29	24	29	11	7	6	3	4	1		2								298
3	5	44	52	61	66	42	30	21	24	15	7	7	1	1	2	1			1	1				381
4			5	22	39	48	45	38	43	24	17	14	5	5	5	4								314
5				5	18	42	49	36	37	23	22	22	8	6	1		3	1		1		1		275
6					3	23	40	30	29	28	26	12	13	8	4	3	1	1						221
7						5	18	36	30	26	26	13	15	7	6	4	1	1						188
8							5	22	20	30	23	27	12	13	4	3	1		2			1		163
9								2	12	21	18	20	13	5	9	4		2	1		1			108
10									12	9	18	11	13	8	7	2	1			1				82
11										4	10	12	10	20	6	5	2	1		1	1	1		73
12											2	7	13	10	8	6	4	1	1					52
13												2	3	3	7	7	3	5		1	1		1	33
14													4	7	4	1	1	4						21
15														1	1	4	1	1	2		1			11
16																3	4	1						8
17																			2	1				3
18																			1	1				2
20																					1			1
21																						1		1
Grand Total	14	108	155	174	222	237	227	228	210	179	164	113	102	71	50	28	20	10	10	5	3	2	2	2334

Here's the deal. If I had taken the time to look up which statistics I needed to run in order to actually come to definite conclusions, you would still be waiting for this post for the next 10 years. So consider all my commentary as overall impressions and not scientific fact, please.

Impression: The attrition rate at age 20 is really high. In fact the number of horses drops to such a small number at age 20, the "average season" probably doesn't mean much at that point and beyond. There just isn't a big enough sample size. (Number of horses in each age group can be seen in the bottom row of the data table.)

Impression: There aren't any horses older than 18 starting endurance for the first time in this data set. In fact, once you hit the mid-teens, most horses tend to have at least one season under their belts (girths?). Look at the blank cells in the top row.

Bottom line? Horses can be successful into their 20s, and definitely their teens, but if they aren't already in the sport by their mid-teens odds are they won't be doing the sport at all. Considering that these numbers include LD's and don't differentiate between LD's and endurance distances (50-mile rides and beyond) makes this even more striking. Those mid-teen horses aren't even starting LD careers.

Of course I couldn't stop there.

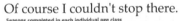

Seasons completed in each individual age class

Above: Percentages are calculated in COLUMNS. i.e. each column adds up to 100 percent.

The gray area near the bottom of the chart is the seasons that are not possible for that age group to achieve.

Impression: Starting in the mid-teens, horses no longer are achieving maximum number of seasons possible based on their age, represented by blank cells in the above table that border the gray area. It's hard to know whether it's because they started the sport later than 4 or 5-years-old, or whether it's because the horses are skipping seasons later on. Probably a combination of both.

The light-green cells[40] represent how many seasons completed the majority of the age group aligns with. I admit that I eyeballed it, but I went back and checked averages and standard deviations. My guesses represented by the green cells are pretty close. This confirms what the first graph showed us, that average number of seasons increases with age. However, what's remarkable is how tight that distribution center remains all the way through.

Impression: If a horse hasn't started completing seasons by the time it is 9 or 10-years-old, it remains in the minority for its age class, even if it continues to complete rides every year until it's 20. I have a hard time wrapping my head around what this means. It seems to suggest that if you want to be doing endurance on your horse when it's 19 or 20-years-old, the best way to make that happen is to start this sport when that horse is between the ages of 8 to 11-years-old, NOT older, like 13 or 15-years-old. Wear-and-tear may matter less than the superior physiological adaptation of younger horses compared to older horses experiencing the same stresses for the first time.

---

40. *Upper light-gray cells in versions of the manuscript not in color.*

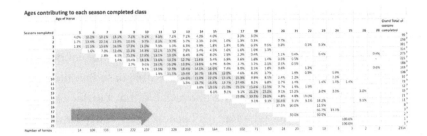

Above: Same table as before, except now the percentages are calculated in ROWS (seasons). Each row adds up to 100 percent.

I, of course, couldn't help compare where Farley fits into this data. Rather predictably Farley started this sport as a younger horse of 8 or 9-years-old, continues to be successful into her teens, AND I already had a gut feeling that endurance after age 20 was a step into the great unknown, something I feel is confirmed in this data. In fact, she is firmly in a green cell based on years of age and seasons indicating that we are indeed quite *average.

*I guess it says something that she certainly doesn't feel average. She feels exceptional. Which is probably more a function of starting this sport on a non-Arabian which was SO HARD, and because Farley is a fun, safe, little packer who showed a knack for 100s and let me achieve my Tevis dream. So in the details she is special, but not so much in the big picture.

So let's talk about decade team.

The problem with this data set is that it counts seasons made up entirely of LD miles as a completed season, which does not count towards the official decade team[41] designation. And it's impossible to tell whether the miles and seasons are being completed by the

---

41. *AERC rules when this volume was published.*

same rider. But let's ignore that and see what the data says about horses completing 10 seasons anyways!

Impression: While there was a pretty clear drop-off of horses over the age of 19-years-old in the sport, it's less clear where the maximum number of seasons is, probably because the age of the horse is a more important factor than the number of seasons. Possibly 14 seasons? Which would correlate to a 19-year-old horse that started this sport around 5-years-old.

Impression: 15-year-olds are the biggest contributor to decade team, and there is a significant drop in horses achieving 10 seasons after 17 years of age. This again suggests that a large number of seasons are achieved by horses that start out in this sport relatively early.

What do you think? I think it would be AWESOME to have the time and knowledge to be able to calculate how likely a horse is to still be doing endurance at age 20 depending on what age they start in endurance (probably some sort of odds or risk ratio), but that would require a far more complicated data set then this one, and more time and brain power than I currently possess. Sigh. That's the problem. Satisfying one's curiosity only leads to more questions!

The More You Know, the Less You Need

"THE MORE YOU know, the less you need"

I came across this saying as I was doing research into ideas for an ultralight backpacking trip I'll be taking this summer.

It rings true. Let's consider the three stages in an active sport like endurance or backpacking, completely made up by me of course. Your mileage may vary, but I bet more than a few of you have experienced the same thing!

Stage 1. You bring a moderate amount of stuff, but it's all the wrong stuff.

Stage 2. You add a bunch of stuff to your kit, and now you have way too much stuff, some of the right stuff, but some of the wrong stuff too, left over from stage 1.

Stage 3. You get rid of a bunch of stuff and now you have relatively little stuff.

In stage 3, the amount of stuff has been reduced, either because a). You never used it, it expired, and you realized that you wouldn't know how to use it if you did have to. Or:

b). It was redundant. Or…

c). It was totally unnecessary.

Another factor that may contribute to the Marie Kondo purging of your gear in stage 3 is that you are less likely to make mistakes that would require a plethora of stuff, and thus you can weed out some of that gear that was there to protect you if you did something really stupid. However, often this backfires, and you enter the optional stage 4.

Stage 4. Slightly more stuff than stage 3. Usually a result of getting yourself in trouble in using a kit that was too minimalist, so you've added some gear back in.

You can tell what "stage" someone is in by the stories they tell when they come back from a ride or a trip.

Stage 1: OMG everything went wrong and I had to totally improvise something out of baling twine because I had everything EXCEPT an extra stirrup leather in my crew bag.

Stage 2: Nothing went wrong but I was totally prepared and had my crew haul two extra tack boxes to every check!!!!!!! Since I don't have a story, let me tell you how prepared and organized I was!

Stage 3: OMG you would never believe the wacky thing that went wrong!!!! I totally used baling twine that I found on my neighbors trailer to fashion a breast collar so that I could finish the ride! Maybe I should throw a stirrup leather back into my crew box. That particular piece of equipment can double as a breast collar, stirrup leather, rein, girth — multi-useful!

In endurance, I'm probably still transitioning from stage 2 to stage 3. I've weeded out a lot of my necessary stuff, but I have yet to have something truly horrible to happen that requires me to rethink my kit. On the other hand, I probably still couldn't do a cavalry ride easily (completing an endurance ride with only the equipment you have with you or you can find on the trail).

A much more fun and obvious example of the proverb is backpacking.

Backpacking illustrates the stages very well because the motivation to go with less is very high. The more you have, the more unpleasant is that trek up that very long, steep hill. You don't stay in stage 2 for very long!

But the motivation for being prepared is also high since it can be very uncomfortable, not to mention life-threatening, to make a bad decision and leave something at home you actually need.

I'm not going to bore you with my stage 1 and 2 experiences backpacking. It was a predictable trajectory driven by balancing the comfort of a light weight load with the enjoyment of camp once the dang pack is off my back. (Pillow? Light, but takes up space, but oh so comfy! Camera? Book? Comfy Therma-rest or lighter mylar blanket?)

Much more entertaining is the incident that marked my move from stage 3 to stage 4.

By a certain New Year's Day backpacking trip I was firmly in the stage 3 of backpacking. I had detailed lists of what I had taken on previous backpacking trips, what was actually used, and how much was used. With these lists I had pared down my kit until only those items that I actually needed and used were included. I wasn't stupid. I still brought matches even though I had never used them. Same for the emergency poncho and such, but in general I had reduced and eliminated my kit to the barest of necessities, and it was gloriously light.

And then — disaster. On a sub-freezing evening only a single day into the trip I got up to pee. I ummm, "misused," my umm, "body-water director," and dumped a certain body fluid down the inside of my pants, completely soaking my undergarments, long underwear, pants, and socks.

Not a big deal, you say? Change into your spare clothes, you say?

In the interest of weight I had no spare clothes. Just spare socks because after all, this is stage 3, not stage 1 and I know enough to at least carry spare socks in a ziplock and a mylar blanket in case something like this happened. Because of the cold temperatures that evening I was wearing every single layer I had brought, each layer being perfectly planned as to not overlap each other in function.

Thus I found myself with a dog, in a 15-degree sleeping bag, (which I will argue was absolutely not a 15-degree bag) without an insulating ground pad (to reduce weight), wearing dry socks. Temperatures were in the single digits that night. A single digit morning followed.

I was fairly miserable. And cold. And pathetic.

Not dead, not dying, but uncomfortable enough that I learned my lesson. Minimalist is nice, and while it was true I needed less stuff than when I first started, and I was prepared enough that my situation wasn't life-threatening (extra socks for the win). But how much weight would it have really added to throw in an extra pair of silkweight leggings? At the cost of a few ounces if they hadn't been needed, I could have been quite comfortable even in the face of my stupidity.

Let's share!!!!!!!!

I would love to hear any good stories that illustrate your journey through the stages, but I know that writing up a story takes time. So, here's an alternative. I thought we could swap the following sentence completions.....

I always bring _____(1)_____ to a ride/trip because I always end up using it!

I used to bring _____(2)_____, but now I leave it at home because I've never needed it, and in some cases, after some reflection, it was kind of ridiculous anyways.

After some "interesting" experiences I've added ____(3)_____ to my equipment list, even if I don't use it regularly.

Ready?

Here's some of mine.

1.

- Spare reins. Three pairs of reins broke in my second season.

- Garbage bag. A multitude of uses including segregating nasty things from the rest of my kit, insurance in case my water bladder leaks in my pack, as an emergency poncho, and as a ground cloth. If I haven't used it by the end of the ride, I can always use it for manure!

- Extra water bottles. I've done two rides to date where water bottles were damaged or lost, and I didn't have spares. I'm also known for not cleaning my water bottles and then realizing that they are full of mold once I arrive at the ride.

- A towel. I undervalued the towel on both rides and backpacking trips early on, but I LOVE having one and use it almost every trip.

2.

- Book or magazine. I love reading but usually can't concentrate or enjoy reading anything at endurance rides or on trips. A bottle of wine is much more amusing and engaging and has the bonus of engaging other people.

- Anything that requires more cooking than simply boiling water

- Heart rate monitor

- GPS

- Duct tape. It never does what I want it to do, breaks down in the heat, and doesn't stick in the cold.

- Extra batteries.[42] I put new batteries in my headlamp at home before the trip if I think that they are going to need to be changed. If the camera goes dead, oh well. More applicable to backpacking than endurance riding. When possible I choose equipment that doesn't need batteries.

3.

- "Quik clot" pack, ace bandage (all sorts of uses), water-treatment pills[43] (small bottle), feminine pads for wound bandages

---

42. *Since writing this post several years ago, batteries (and GPS) rotate on and off the list. Depending on exactly where I'm going and what I'm doing they are either essentials, or not.*

43. *Now I carry in an inline water filter that can screw onto a bottle or can be used like a straw.*

25 Things

HEADING OFF TO your first LD of 25 miles or more? Feeling a bit nervous? Relax! Here's 25 of the essential must-knows[44] before, and after, pulling into ridecamp.

1. Know where ridecamp is.

Ridecamps are often in the middle of nowhere without addresses or readily GPS'ed cross streets. Sometimes you are given GPS coordinates and sometimes step-by-step directions. YAY! And sometimes you aren't. Sometimes you aren't even warned there are TWO streets of the same name, and the SECOND one is your turn-off, and it could result in having to backtrack through a residential section by backing your truck and trailer[45] a quarter mile before being able to turn around. (True story) Best is to have at least two methods of navigation to ridecamp — Written step-by-step directions and/or GPS and/or area map, etc.

---

44. *This is a reprint of an article that originally appeared on my blog in June 2015. If you've read this far, you will probably recognize the back-story on many of these nuggets of advice!*

45. *Have you read the chapter on backing a trailer yet? Have you practiced?*

2. Know and understand the AERC rules.

It's tricky. Gate-and-goes versus gate-into-holds, who has to weigh with tack, and finish criteria guidelines. The specifics will be discussed at the ride, but you should be very familiar with the most current AERC handbook before coming to ridecamp.

3. Read the ride flyer completely.

This will prevent all sorts of misunderstandings from whether you should leave your dog at home, to what kinds of containment systems are allowed for your horse.

4. If required, find and purchase weed-free hay.

How do you know whether you need it? See #3.

5. Be prepared to pay camping fees, if any, at the ride site.

(Have you done #3 yet?)

6. Take each moment as it comes and try to let go of preconceived notions.

I can't emphasize this enough. You have probably been day-dreaming about this moment for months. More likely than not you have some sort of image or expectation of how the event will go. Maybe it's what your camp will look like, or how the ride will be organized, or how your fellow riders will act and behave. Here's the reality. You've been in love with an idea. Now is the time to experience the reality, the good, the wonderful, the transformative, and well, the bad and ugly too. For your first ride go into the event with as blank a slate as possible. You've been told the ride is well-organized, cool, with minimal hills, and has a reputation for being short. This year it's record-high temperatures, the trail is actually a bit long, you happen to be surrounded by a group of cranky riders, and the ride manager seems a bit frazzled and distracted every time you see her. It happens. Even today, with over a thousand miles under my belt, when I go to a ride I've never been to before I'm doing so with an open mind to see how this particular ride does things. I'd rather be pleasantly surprised than bitterly disappointed. Each ride tends to have its own unique flavor, and that's OK!

7. Bring more horse food then you think you will need.

My horses eat double the amount of hay during a ride than they do at home!

8. There will be a ride meeting.

Sit up front if you want to hear what is being said. And you do. People in the back tend to whisper and talk. Rude? Probably. But instead of spending your time annoyed and frustrated and shushing everyone, just plan on sitting up front. Don't worry when the ride manager inevitably starts rattling off random trail information, and you go, "Huh?" because you don't know what water trough on last year's figure-8 loop was that they are changing this year. Just go with the flow. Focus on ribbon colors, how the trail and turns are marked, where and how long the holds are, is tack on or off for vet checks, what is the pulse criteria and time criteria for holds and finish, whether there are any unique things about the ride, such as needing to pick up tokens at certain parts of the trail to prove you travelled the distance. Lastly, pay attention to where are crewbags being sent, and are there any special requirements such as send hay, DON'T send hay, or bring your own rider food? That covers most of the important information.

9. Pre-plan the crew bag.

There's never as much time as you think in the evening after settling in, eating dinner, going to the ride meeting, and tying up loose ends. Make your life a little less hectic by either pre-packing most of your crew bag or having a comprehensive list.

10. Have a reliable way to get up in the morning.

I've almost missed three ride starts because my alarm was unreliable. My phone's alarm doesn't always work when there's no reception, my watch that I always wake up to at home doesn't even nudge my unconsciousness, the friend that was supposed to wake me up oversleeps. Find something reliable, and then have a back-up too!

11. Resolve to have fun.

Enjoyment and happiness are choices. Being committed to #6 will help. Find a way to make that first ride fun, even if it pours, you get pulled at the first check, wait three hours to get trailered out, and then get stuck in the mud. Or if you are forgotten about on the trail since you are woefully overtime, run out of water, and puke on the side of the trail from heat and exhaustion, only to finally come into the check that is packing up and find that all the human water is gone. Even in those circumstances there can be a sliver of fun. The trail was beautiful, the bond between you and the horse is stronger, the beer afterwards tasted REALLY good, and you know the 14 things you need to change between now and your next ride.

12. Whatcha going to do with your ride card?

Stick it in a baggie and stuff it in a saddle bag? Keep it in your bra? A pocket? A neck thingy?

13. Memorize your rider number.

Ideally, do that before you have to go up to the number-taker at the beginning of the ride and call it out. Early-morning gymnastics in the saddle as you twist and turn to try to read the smeared grease on the horse's butt is less than desirable.

14. Expect your horse to be more naughty than it's ever been on a conditioning ride.

"But he always...!" "But I never have to..." Yeah, but if a ride was the same as conditioning, you would save a lot of time and money by just riding at home. Remember #6? A ride is different than conditioning. Expect your horse to surprise you, pleasantly and umm, not so pleasantly. It's part of the excitement and pleasure of doing a real endurance ride! Being prepared will help a lot.

15. Have a plan for the start BEFORE the morning of the ride.

Are you going to start at the back? In the middle? With a buddy? Pro tip: Don't expect to use another person's horse as a "brake." You slam into the back of my horse because you can't control yours and we are NOT friends.

16. Bring a well-prepared mount. Not just a well-conditioned one.

Be able to handle the most typical trail obstacles that you will probably encounter: Water, single track, gates, cows. Sure, your horse that crosses water at home might turn into a completely different beast (see #6) and refuse to cross water at the ride. But don't bring a horse that doesn't cross water to a ride known for its water crossings and expect the riders around you to get your horse to cross. Being ready for an endurance ride is more than just covering time and distance. It is about being able to handle the other rigors of the trail as well.

17. Have a plan, but don't expect everything to go to plan...

...and decide how you are going to handle unexpected and last-minute changes.

18. Bring a change of clothes for the half-way point, just in case.

19. Have a solution for unexpected horse footwear malfunctions.

Will there be a farrier? Could you tack on a spare shoe if needed? Are you going to carry a boot? Does it fit?

20. Don't yell or become short-tempered with the ride vets, manager, or volunteers.

For that matter, extend the same courtesy to your fellow riders. Make that commitment now. If you tend to be a volatile person, pre-plan your reactions NOW. Endurance is an incredibly small community, and your reputation starts at your very first endurance ride. Just. Don't. Do. It.

21. Bring a variety of food for you!

I'm a person who loves food and eats plenty of it. Other events such as long distance running are ALL ABOUT THE EATING. But when it comes to endurance rides I have a really tough time eating. Nothing sounds good, a wrong choice leaves me gagging and dry-heaving, and I'd prefer to skip the whole eating thing altogether. I pack lots of different stuff in small quantities. The round and rectangle lunch-box-sized plastic containers work well. Having LOTS of different options in front of me to sample at ridecamp and vet checks also makes a difference. I'm not a huge junk-food eater, but at rides the most delicious, addicting junk-foods, as well as my favorite non-junk foods, go in the food box. I pack things that are so addicting that if I eat them at home I can't stop eating until they are gone. THAT is the kind of food I pack for ridecamp. Ham and cheese sandwiches, peanut butter M&Ms[46], SmartFood white cheddar popcorn, Gaslight kettle corn, animal crackers, a certain brand of pork skins, mac and cheese with tuna, Hershey almond and chocolate drops, Stoats bars, pizza, rice pudding, fresh fruit, etc. I really like freeze-dried backpacking meals, and so packing a couple of those for dinner time helps me get down enough calories

---

46. *Any brandnames mentioned in the text are not endorsements, and I do not have a financial interest in any of these companies. Im merely sharing the specific products that have worked best for me over time.*

in addition to the snacks.

22. Bring at least some human food that doesn't require cooking.

Bring some even if you are planning on bringing a camp stove or similar. Because on this one occasion, despite all my efforts, my camp stove would NOT work. I looked around in dismay at all the food I had brought and realized that everything I had either needed to be heated or have hot water added to it to make it edible. Ugh. Don't be stuck eating crunchy, cold mac and cheese with tuna like me!

23. Bring cash for ride photos.

Some photographers will have proofs available online some time after the ride. Other photographers will have images available at the end of the ride already printed out. Since I never know in advance who is going to be photographing the ride I take $20 for photos, just in case.

24. Have an idea of what resources and actions you would be willing to do if your horse needs treatment at a ride.

Of all the AERC official distances, statistics show you are the least likely to be pulled and/or require treatment after an LD. However, strange things happen, and riding endurance at any distance is not without risk. If you make the decision to expose your horse to a greater risk of illness and injury, such as riding in competitions, you owe it to your mount to be able to do some basic care if needed. Thinking about basic guidelines right now will help you and the vet make decisions more efficiently if needed. What is your budget? Will you trailer out to the referral hospital or treat on-site only? Is colic surgery an option? Don't worry, vets don't expect that everyone will be able to have surgery done!

25. Bring something to clean up and take home manure.

Not all rides will require this, and not all rides that require this will make it clear on the ride flyer. Best to be prepared just in case. I find that heavy-duty trash bags and a manure fork is the best method, and they don't take up a lot of space in case I don't end up using them.

50 Things

FIFTY MILES INVOLVES a little more homework and preparation than an LD, but it's worth it. Here's 25 more things to get you to your first 50-mile ride.

26. Different regions have different norms.

When traveling outside your normal region, take some time to find someone familiar with the region and ask some questions about what you can expect and what customs might be different.

27. Spend some time before the ride listening to gut sounds.

Know what's normal for your horse. Don't rely on the letter grades from the vet cards.

28. Learn how to…

…back your own trailer. Have you been practicing the tips from the previous chapter?

29. Figure out the best horse containment.

Figure it out for you, your horse, and the ride you will be attending. Every system has its pros and cons. Not every ridecamp can accommodate all systems. Something as simple as "tie to the trailer" can work!

30. Think about treatment (again).

The longer the ride distance, the higher the chance of something going WRONG. You may be very careful, ride smart, and be prepared, and still be faced with the decision of whether or how to treat your horse at a ride. Yes, this is a repeat from the first 25. Don't think it won't happen to you!

31. Do your homework.

Research the most common diseases and conditions of endurance horses so if it happens to you, and it will eventually, you can make informed decisions. Learn about colic in the endurance horse which is different than your "normal" colic, as well as tying-up, muscle cramps, thumps, rock bruises, and bowed tendons.

32. Evaluate past performances.

Write down three things that went really well and three things that didn't from every ride you've done so far, whether you've finished or not. Address problems and don't abandon things that have worked well.

33. Bust training myths.

You don't need to do 50 miles in training before your first 50. You don't need to do 50 miles in a week before you do your first 50.

34. Invest in rain gear.

Good rain gear. Wet and cold for 25 miles is different from wet, cold, and tired over 50 miles.

35. Prepare for heat.

You won't be done by lunch time!

36. Peeing on the trail. Figure it out.

37. Consider finding a mentor.

Think about this if you haven't already. You don't absolutely need one, but it will make things easier. The person you choose doesn't have to be available in real life. Email, messaging, and phone calls work too.

38. Prepare for darkness.

Depending on the time of year, you may have to do parts of the trail in the dark. Carry a headlamp if the 12-hour finish time ends after dusk.

39. Simplify your gear.

Purge anything not necessary. This includes most of your just-in-case stuff.

40. Ask someone to crew.

Even if you feel you eventually won't need a crew for the 50-mile distance, it might make your first 50 more fun and doable.

41. Have a pacing plan.

The longer the distance, the more that little mistakes add up and amplify. I'm consistently a midpack, top-third finisher and for what it's worth, my pacing plan never includes planned cantering or starting with the pack. Walk/trot is more than sufficient to finish the distance under cutoffs. Don't bank time in the beginning. Keep it down to a dull roar from the very beginning.

42. RELAX.

Mental stress and anxiety will decrease the amount of mental and physical effort you will have at your disposal on ride day. So chill the frick out.

43. Ride your own ride.

Don't depend on riding with someone else for the duration of the ride.

44. Ride well.

It doesn't have to be show-ring perfect. It does have to be efficient and not make your horse's job harder, or impossible.

45. Expect low points during the ride.

Expect them for both you and your horse. Sometimes they'll happen at the same time and sometimes not. It's normal and doesn't necessarily mean you aren't ready for the distance! Especially for a horse that knows the LD distance really well the first 50 can be a wake-up call.

46. Grumpiness = eat something.

If you find yourself in the pit of despair it's probably because you need to eat something. Trust me. If you feel like you are just going to puke it up, eat anyways. What's the worst that will happen? Puke? No big deal.

47. It's going to be hard(er).

At your first 50-mile ride, and beyond, expect things to go wrong. It won't be easy and it won't be what you expect. I read a lot of greenbean posts, and I think the common theme is that they don't expect it to be as hard as it is. Training is perhaps going well, giving them a false idea of how the real deal will go, and they expect ride management and the other riders to somehow make it easier for them. It's hard for everyone.

48. Don't give up.

Each longer distance carries a higher risk of failure. It's worth sticking with and doing!

49. Be a newbie, again.

Don't be surprised if moving up a distance makes you feel like you have to figure it all out again. Doesn't mean you aren't ready, and doesn't mean you did anything wrong before. It's a humbling sport!

50. Smell the roses.

Fifty miles is a long way, but even over the course of 12 hours it's amazing how we forget to look at the scenery, give the horse a pat on the neck, and give thanks for everything that went together well enough so that we managed to make it at least to the start line. Try to ride each mile like it's the last one on your beloved equine partner, because sometimes it is. Stop worrying about the miles ahead or the drama behind you. Just be in the mile you are riding right now.

The End

NOW, GO RIDE, and I'll see you on the trails!

Did you know that most books are sold through word of mouth?

I need your help.

I love writing, sharing the best stories, and making my work available for less than a cup of decent coffee.

If you enjoyed this book, will you please....

1. **Recommend** it to a friend
2. **Share** on social media
3. **Leave a review** on Amazon
4. **Check out my blog**, read hundreds of posts for free, and sign up for my (very infrequent) newsletter.

Thank you!
Dr. Melinda Newton
The running, riding, writing veterinarian

Website: www.drmelnewton.com
Email: Mel@drmelnewton.com
Facebook: Facebook.com/drmelnewton
Instagram: Instragram.com/drmelnewton

Other Books by Dr. Mel Newton

The Running, Riding, Writing Veterinarian Series

Go Ride Far: Practical know-how from the running, riding, writing veterinarian

Bar Napkin Guides

Play Any Instrument: A guide for adults who don't want to learn theory or take lessons. A Bar Napkin Guide by Orvetta Black[47]

---

47. *Dr. Mel's pen name*

Melinda Newton, DVM is a veterinary practitioner and free-lance writer who lives in Northern California with her husband, daughter, and (according to her husband) too many animals. She loves a good story and lots of miles on the trail. Whether it's on horseback or on her own two feet, Dr. Mel's favorite distance is 100 miles. Is there anything more wonderful than running all day and night, and then spending the rest of the day napping on the couch? Her husband isn't convinced and makes her get her own snacks when she wakes up, since any pain and soreness is self-induced. Dr. Mel been telling stories about running, riding, and veterinary medicine on her blog since 2009. Her mission is simple: Inspire and motivate readers to go out and do exciting things that make life richer even if they seem impossible. It is the little steps and choices every day that culminate into your dreams. Dr. Newton also writes under the pen name of Orvetta Black, and is the author of the Bar Napkin Guide books, and numerous nationally published articles.

Looking for your next book?

A Bar Napkin Guide: Play Any Instrument

Do you have an instrument that you've always dreamed of playing? Is your Grandma's piano sitting in your living room unused? You are only one little book away from playing any instrument. Learn the essentials of music and start playing now.

Bar Napkin Guides are the essential how-to for the new skill you want to learn. It's just like friends scribbling the must-do's on a napkin during a night out. Except this one won't end up crumbled in your jean pocket and in the wash, and the handwriting is easier to read in the morning. This Bar Napkin covers:

- Picking the right instrument (with three recommendations)
- How to connect the dots between your instrument, a fingering chart, and the music in front of you
- Other useful tools like metronomes and tuners
- Specific tasks at the end of each chapter to keep you on track

    ...and more!

"This book is a MUST READ for anyone wanting to learn to play an instrument (or anyone wanting to enroll their children in music lessons). The author really strips away the "musician's lingo" and reveals what all of those words and terms mean, in a very common sense, understandable way. I've been playing a few instruments (on a basic level) for years, but this book was enlightening to me and explained a lot of things that I do, but didn't know why I did them (someone just told me "you do it this way" and I went with it). Now I can understand the framework..."
~Amy V.

Read on for a sample from Play Any Instrument...

Available as an ebook or paperback from select online retailers. Learn more at drmelnewton.com

A BAR NAPKIN GUIDE: PLAY ANY INSTRUMENT

BY ORVETTA BLACK

The guide for adults who don't want to learn theory or take lessons

Introduction

Playing music is worthy of your time. By picking up this book I'm making the assumption you agree with me. But just in case, consider just how special playing music is. It connects, entertains, challenges, and relaxes. It can be done by yourself or in a community of people. Like food, music is a universal language.

Learning music is good for our brains. At its essence learning music is about breaking down large amounts of new complex information into small doable chunks, a concept that can be applied to many other situations. There are multiple studies showing the benefit of musical education in children, but adults will benefit too. Researchers at Johns Hopkins University found that older adults who took a few piano lessons had improvements in the areas of attention, memory, problem-solving abilities, moods, and quality of life. In both children and adults, playing music improves executive function. Executive function is a high-level cognitive process by the brain that enables us to quickly process and retain information, make good choices, solve problems, and adapt to changing tasks. Sounds like excellent skills to cultivate!

Playing with other people increases cooperation, improves the sense of community, and reduces depression. Music is the ultimate practice of mindfulness that is all the craze right now. Sitting still and being quiet not your thing? I promise you that it is almost impossible not to be fully in the moment as you tackle a piece of music. Everything else fades away.

Two simple music lessons and five tasks; that is the difference between having no experience with music, and being able to read music notation and play an instrument! This book will walk you through these steps.

Your First Instrument

Choosing your first instrument is like agreeing to a blind date. Likely, if you are reading this book, you already have an instrument in mind, but that doesn't mean you shouldn't consider other candidates. Remember, it's unlikely that the first instrument you learn will be the only one you ever learn. Choosing an easier instrument for a first instrument means faster progress now, which means starting your next (and more difficult) instrument well-prepared and armed with the concepts you've already learned.

What makes an instrument easy or hard to learn? What are the characteristics of a good first instrument? I have strong opinions of which you should start with, but first, let's meet the potential candidates for your first musical date.

Cost, quality, and the beginner

Some instruments cost more than others. As a beginner you don't want to pay a fortune for an instrument only to find out after a few months you really don't like it very much and want to move on. But, you also need an instrument of good enough quality that you can play it! Cheap beginner instruments are sometimes so difficult to play that even an expert has trouble making them sound good and getting them to work properly.

Ideally you want an affordable instrument of mid-quality. Depending on the instrument, this may mean buying used or new. For example, a soprano recorder is a woodwind instrument that has been played for hundreds of years, and is still a versatile and relevant instrument today. A new soprano recorder of mid-level quality is extremely affordable. Most instruments you see in school band (trumpets, flutes, clarinets) can be found used of decent quality and for reasonable prices.

....Continued in "Play Any Instrument"

Check it out!

https://www.drmelnewton.com/Bar-Napkin-Guide-Play-Any-Instrument

Made in the USA
Coppell, TX
19 March 2023